FOOD AND SOCI

1.

'Banquetting Stuffe'

'Banquetting Stuffe'

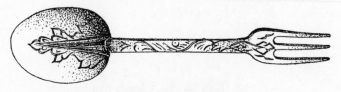

The fare and social background of the Tudor and Stuart banquet

EDITED BY C. ANNE WILSON

with illustrations by
Peter Brears

Edinburgh University Press

Papers from the First Leeds Symposium
on Food History and Traditions,
April 1986

© C. Anne Wilson, 1991
Edinburgh University Press
22 George Square, Edinburgh

Set in Berthold Garamond
by Hislop & Day Limited, Edinburgh
and printed in Great Britain by
The Alden Press Limited, Oxford

British Library Cataloguing
in Publication Data
'Banquetting stuffe':
the fare and social background of the
Tudor and Stuart banquet.—(Food and society, 1).
1. Great Britain. Banquets. Social aspects, history
I. Wilson, C. Anne (Constance Anne). II. Series
394.1'5

ISBN 0 7486 0103 1

Contents

About the contributors

PETER BREARS is the Director of Leeds City Museums. He combines his interests in archaeology, architecture and the traditional food of Northern England with a great deal of practical experience of recreating the culinary confections of earlier centuries.

LYNETTE HUNTER is a Lecturer at the University of Leeds' Institute of Bibliography and Textual Criticism. She has published several books and articles on modern English literature, and is general editor of *Household and Cookery Books Published in Britain* 1800-1914.

JENNIFER STEAD trained as an art historian and writes on social history and food history. Her publications include *Food and Cooking in 18th Century Britain*.

ANNE WILSON has worked for many years in the Brotherton Library of the University of Leeds, becoming involved in food history as a result of cataloguing the John Preston Collection of early English cookery books. This led to *Food and Drink in Britain from the Stone Age to Recent Times*. She is currently researching the very early history of distilling.

List of illustrations

1. Title-page of *A Closet for Ladies and Gentlewomen* 1611.
2. Engraved title-page of H. Woolley, *The Accomplisht Ladys Delight* 1686. The two pictures above the title show candying and distilling.
3. Title-page from Sir Hugh Platt, *Delightes for Ladies* 1609 edition.
4. A recipe for candying from Sir Hugh Platt, *Delightes for Ladies*.
5. How to make 'collops of bacon' from marchpane stuffe; and walnuts, cinnamon sticks, cards and 'kissing comfits' from sugar-plate.
6. How to model eggs, round cakes and ribbons from sugar-plate.
7. Creams and jellies for the banquet.
8. Designs for 'cut-laid' tarts.
9. Biscuits for the banquet.
10. Late seventeenth-century gingerbread moulds.
11. Sweetmeat glasses, notched lemon slice, and oakleaf and plum modelled from stiff marmalade.
12. Elevation and plan of the banquet table from F. Massialot, *New Instructions for Confectioners* 1702 edition.
13. Roundels with poesies, and sucket forks with spoon ends.
14. (a) Sir William Sharington's Tower, Lacock Abbey, Wiltshire 1549–53.
    (b) Banqueting House, Barlborough Hall, Derbyshire, 1587.
    (c) Banqueting House, built for Sir Francis Newport's 'Great House', Eyton-on-Severn, Shropshire, in 1607.

1.

Introduction:
The Origin of 'Banquetting Stuffe'

Many a visitor who spends a happy Saturday or Sunday afternoon exploring a stately home and its extensive grounds will begin by admiring the great house and its furnishings, and will then turn to the outbuildings and the garden buildings — laundry, ice-house, possibly a folly or two forming a viewpoint at the end of a vista, and the banqueting house. Perhaps it is the banqueting house which is most puzzling. Its situation may be delightful, but why is it so far from the kitchen? Were the great feasts of our forebears really carried out across the gardens to be consumed in this small, idyllic, but often apparently unheated, building?

The fact that such thoughts can cross the mind of even the generally well-informed person gives some indication of how completely the concept of the Tudor and Stuart banquet has dropped out of present-day experience. One reason is the confusion of names between the banquet which was based upon 'banquetting stuffe' and the large, rich dinner which is conjured up by such terms as 'the Lord Mayor's banquet', or is looked for at the 'Banqueting Rooms' in a major town today.

In Tudor and Stuart times the word 'banquet' already had two meanings, one of which implied an opulent meal or great feast, as it does now. But the other meaning was that of the special final course of such a meal, comprising a wide variety of sweetmeats, and it is with this little-known 'banquet' that the chapters of this book are concerned.

So important was the banquet course that it was given its own separate venue. In winter the participants might withdraw from the great chamber or the dining parlour to another room; but for summer banquets individual banqueting houses were designed, built usually in places where the banqueters could take extra pleasure in the surrounding views. The banquet also had its own large repertoire of specialised recipes, given their particular section within contemporary cookery books, or gathered into separate books devoted entirely to 'banquetting stuffe'.

Several historic circumstances led to the adoption of the 'banquet' as the fashionable way in which to end a meal. The medieval feast had concluded with hippocras [spiced wine] and wafers, served separately after the remains of the dishes of the final main course had been carried away. But at that final (second, or occasionally third) main course, some sweet dishes were present among the savoury ones, and by the fifteenth century these included such items as the highly decorated almond-paste marchpane. So at this stage a natural preference for finishing a large meal on a sweet note may already have been emerging.

Furthermore, the opportunities were increasing for well-to-do and well-connected people to enjoy sugar-sweetened fare as greater quantities of sugar began to reach Britain. By today's standards the amounts were still modest and its high cost made sugar a luxury readily accessible only to the families of the wealthy and powerful (sugar-loaves were a favourite form of gift or bribe). But, for that very reason, sugar usage became a form of conspicuous consumption; so the idea of a special course dedicated to sugar-based confections was bound to be attractive.

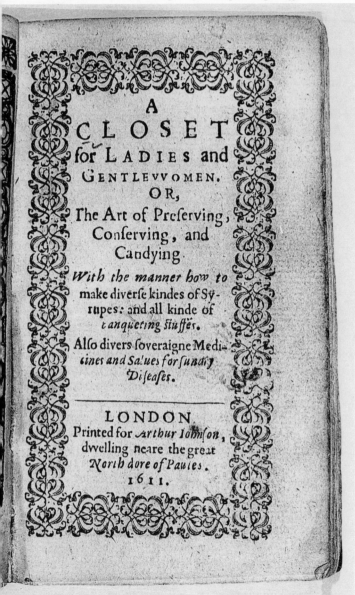

1.
Title-page of
*A Closet for Ladies and
Gentlewomen,* 1611.

A
CLOSET
for LADIES and
GENTLEVVOMEN.
OR,
The Art of Preferving,
Conferving, and
Candying.
With the manner how to
make diverfe kindes of Sy-
rupes: and all kinde of
banquetting ftuffes.
Alfo divers foveraigne Medi-
cines and Salues for fundry
Difeafes.

LONDON,
Printed for *Arthur Iohnfon*,
dwelling neare the great
North dore of Paules.
1611.

Finally, there was the welcome aspect of sugar as a health food, which arose from the medical beliefs of the late middle ages. This view had been handed down from the ancient world: the Greeks and Romans appear to have known sugar only as a medicine. It was the Arabs who extended its use as an ingredient of prepared foodstuffs. But the medical usage continued to be recommended by Arab physicians; and when it first arrived in Western Europe sugar was known mainly as a warming medicine, helpful as a digestive, and a cure for colds. It was eaten not exactly neat, but nearly so, in the form of sugar-plate flavoured with rosewater or spices. The digestive aspects of medicinal sugar naturally encouraged its use at the end of a feast of rich and heavy dishes.

At this stage in the history of sugar the development of a separate final course, where sugared 'banquetting stuffe' could be displayed, admired, and consumed along with spiced wine or flavoured spirits, was perhaps inevitable. And the costliness of the sugar itself ensured that it took place among the well-to-do, who found in the banquet a new area in which to demonstrate to friends and relatives their wealth, their taste, and their appreciation of the latest fashions. It is significant that it was the lady of the house who was at the forefront when it came to producing the 'banquetting stuffe', and not the cook (who in larger households was almost always a man). It was she, assisted by her daughters and maids, who gathered the necessary garden produce and carried out the sugar-work in the stillroom. It was she to whom were addressed the specialised recipe handbooks with titles such as *Delightes for Ladies* and *A Daily Exercise for Ladies and Gentlewomen*.

The summer banquet was given a new exciting setting in the banqueting house, so that the visual pleasure provided by the highly decorative 'banquetting stuffe' was enhanced by that of the distant views over gardens and surrounding scenery. The banquet thus came to have a very strong identity of its own, and there were occasions when a banquet was served in its own right, and not as an adjunct to the main courses of the feast.

Yet by the beginning of the Georgian era, changes in fashion were bringing about the demise of the banquet. The underlying concept survived but it carried as its name the recently adopted French term 'dessert'. And the dishes presented at the dessert displayed subtle changes of emphasis, with creams, jellies, and fresh fruits often predominating, and fewer and less elaborate sugar-works than at the earlier banquet. The dessert, like the banquet, could still be served as a separate course (a custom that continues today in certain circles, for instance at some Oxbridge colleges). But there was a growing tendency to draw it into the environment of the final main course. In the first edition of E. Smith's *The Compleat Housewife* (1727) is a plate bearing a diagram of a table-setting entitled 'Second course, the desert in the middle'. It shows typical second-course fare (wild ducks, rabbits, buttered crabs, peas, artichokes, and lobsters) with an inner group of creams and fruits surrounding 'A pyramid of dry'd sweetmeats' in the centre of the table. The pyramid was an arrangement on a dessert frame of tiers of sweetmeats; such frames became popular among housewives of the middling sort because they took up relatively little space yet provided a colourful centrepiece for the second-course table. The iced and decorated marchpane of marzipan paste, once the centrepiece of the banquet, lost its earlier identity and was transferred to the top of the bridecake and other rich fruitcakes for special occasions.

Thus the banquet met its end. But the curious way in which the word 'banquet', with the particular meaning defined above, disappeared from the English language may have been partly due to the fact that its other sense, that of the sumptuous meal, has neither disappeared nor changed very much through the centuries. Its survival has served to blot out all the more completely the memory of the banquet course; and that may be one reason why historians of the sixteenth and seventeenth centuries have not hitherto done justice to the institution itself, its semiology, and its role in contemporary social life. We hope that the present volume will serve to redress previous neglect.

The first Leeds Symposium on Food History and Traditions was held at the Department of Adult and Continuing Education, University of Leeds, on 26 April, 1986. It was the success of the Oxford Food Symposium, founded in 1979 by Alan Davidson and held annually at St Anthony's College, Oxford, which led me to consider the idea of a food history symposium for the North of England. The Oxford Symposia have a wide remit; those who attend them come from many different parts of the world and include restauranteurs, restaurant critics, food writers, home economists and people professionally concerned with dietetics, as well as food historians. The topics discussed are far-ranging, and symposium members are divided into separate groups to cater for different interests.

In the Brotherton Library at the University of Leeds we are fortunate in having two important collections of early cookery-books: the Blanche Leigh collection of English and Continental books from 1475 to the present day; and the John Preston collection of English books from 1584 to 1861 (the year of the first edition of Mrs Beeton's *The Book of Household Management*). In July 1988 a third collection, the Camden collection of twentieth-century cookery-books to the year 1976, was added to the other two, thus greatly enriching our holdings of more recent books. It was through cataloguing the John Preston collection in the 1960s that I first became interested in food history; and it was through their similar interests that I first met Jennifer Stead (author of *Food and Cooking in Eighteenth-Century Britain*) and Peter Brears, director of Leeds City Museums. When Lynette Hunter joined the School of

English at the University of Leeds, she was already general editor of the bibliographies of nineteenth-century cookery and household books currently being brought out by Prospect Books (D. Attar's *A Bibliography of Household Books published in Britain 1800–1914,* [1988] and E. Driver's *A Bibliography of Cookery Books published in Britain 1875–1914* [1989]) and she knew the Brotherton Library's early cookery-books as an important research resource. Thus there was a small team of people at hand locally, each able to bring special knowledge to bear upon particular aspects of food history in Britain; and we decided to institute a one-day symposium with a single aspect of food history as the focus of each meeting. 'Banquetting Stuffe' was our first topic.

The news of the forthcoming first Leeds Symposium aroused great interest: so many applied to attend that we were obliged to turn some away because the demonstration room used on that occasion could hold no more than sixty people. The demonstration was given by Peter Brears and was one of the highlights of the day. He prepared a great many items of 'banquetting stuffe': marchpanes, gilded, lettered, and struck with comfits; realistic-looking walnut shells of almond paste spiced and browned with cinnamon (made in moulds that were copies of seventeenth-century wooden originals) and containing jelly of quinces; moulded gingerbreads in the form of soldiers of the period; white and coloured leach in a chequered pattern; and many other 'conceited dishes' which caused as much delight in April 1986 as they must have done when the recipes were first tried out; and he explained the practical details of how they were made.

Under his direction, the other members of the team had prepared further jellies, leaches, biscuits, cakes and sweetmeats to add to his contributions, in sufficient quantities to allow sixty people the opportunity to taste most of them. This banquet was laid out with the items in due order as they might have appeared at a banquet of

Elizabethan or Stuart times; and at 5.00 p.m. after the final paper had been presented, the members of the audience were invited to enjoy a glass of spiced wine and to sample the 'banquetting stuffe'.

Unfortunately, the printed word cannot do full justice to either the appearance or the flavours of this re-created banquet. But Peter Brears's chapter, expanded from the practical advice he gave during his demonstration, contains useful recipes to allow anyone who so wishes to carry out a similar re-creation.

We hope each of the chapters in this book will be found interesting in its own right, and that together they will help to rescue from oblivion the significant institution of Tudor and Stuart social life known as the 'banquet'.

C.A.W.
Leeds.
August 1988.

2.

The Evolution of the Banquet Course: Some Medicinal, Culinary and Social Aspects

C. ANNE WILSON

When you and your friends or family have enjoyed a well- **The** cooked meal together, and you have come to the end of **banquet** the final course, you all leave the table and move into easy chairs; or, if your house is so designed, you leave the dining-room altogether and seat yourselves comfortably in the drawing-room. You then offer your companions coffee and a few chocolate mints, or perhaps some other form of chocolate, or candy, or small fancy biscuits. You may not realise it, but this little appendage to the meal represents a late, faint reflection of the Tudor and Stuart banquet. For that was a final course of delicious sweetmeats served after the main meal had been cleared away, sometimes in a specially built banqueting house at a distance from the great house where the rest of the feast had been consumed.

The word 'banquet' used in this context is apt to cause confusion today. We have to remember that the kind of meal which we call a banquet would, in medieval times, and even much later, have been referred to as a feast. Moreover, the confusion goes back almost as far as the time when the word 'banquet' entered the English language. According to the dictionaries, the French word 'banquet' derives from the Italian 'banchetto', which had originally meant a small bench or table but had also taken on the additional sense of a magnificent meal — perhaps

9

initially a very special meal served to a few important people at a small table. It reached England with the meaning of a splendid meal, and first appeared in print in the plural form of 'bankettis' in Caxton's edition of the *Golden Legend* published in 1483.[1]

But within forty years, banquets were being mentioned in contexts which show that the word had already taken on its other meaning: that of a separate course of sweetmeats consumed at the end of the feast. One cannot help wondering whether this other concept also came from Italy, perhaps more directly in connection with the sweetmeats themselves. Several items of what was to become 'banquetting stuffe' (especially the preserved citrus peels, marmalades of quinces, and conserves of soft fruits) were already being produced in Italy in the early sixteenth century, for the secret of their manufacture had by then spread beyond Spain and Portugal. When these Italian delicacies, and perhaps also sugar-candies and little spiced sweet dry cakes of the type which became known as Naples biscuit, arrived at the Port of London along with the sugar and spices on the Venetian and Genoese galleys, they may well have been offered to prospective purchasers as sweetmeats fit for a banquet (in the sense of a feast). But, in practice, they were consumed at a single point in the feast: that is, at the end. Hence, the final course became a feast which crowned the total feast, or a banquet which crowned the main banquet. So, although the derivation of this special English usage of 'banquet' to describe the final course is still a mystery to lexicographers, the suggestion made here could well turn out to be the true answer to the problem: that it was the sweetmeats from southern Europe with their festal association which gave the Tudor and Stuart final course its festal name of 'banquet'.

Concluding the Although there was a great upsurge in the quantity and
medieval feast variety of these imported delicacies during the sixteenth

century, the banquet fare of late Tudor times did not suddenly appear from nowhere. From at least the thirteenth century the feasts of the nobility had by custom concluded with hippocras (sweetened spiced wine) and wafers, served together and on their own, sometimes just before the board was cleared and sometimes afterwards.[2]

At the end of the greatest feasts, those of royalty and the principal noble lords, wine and spices were, on occasion, offered as an additional finale, after the board had been cleared, at a special ceremony called the *voidée* or void. This practice, along with its name, came from France. The chamberlain led forth a procession of household officials bearing magnificently decorated silver and silver-gilt wine-cups and spice-plates from the cupboard where they had been laid out. The royal wine and spices were first assayed (tasted to prove their wholesomeness) by the bearer, and then the king's wine-cup and spice-plate were handed ceremoniously to him; the king might, in turn, offer them to a special guest whom he wished to honour. Thereafter, esquires of the household carried the wine and spices to the rest of the company.[3] Both the ceremonious bringing forth of the sweetmeats ordained for the occasion and the separateness of this part of the meal from what had gone before were to survive to become part of the tradition of the banquet.

The original reason for serving the spices, either in their natural state or sugar-coated, together with the spiced wine at that stage of the meal was, of course, medicinal. The spices chosen were those believed to be warming to the stomach and, therefore, helpful for the digestion of the food consumed at the meal.

By the fifteenth century there are already references to other additions to the customary hippocras and wafers. The list of provisions for the feast when George Nevill was enthroned as Archbishop of York in 1467 closes with 'spices, sugared delicates and wafers plenty', a pipe of

Spices and composts

hippocras having already been included earlier in the list. Again, 'Hot apples and pears with sugar candy/with ginger columbine minced mannerly,/wafers and hippocras' are the fare offered as the final course in a menu for 'A Dinere of Fische' in John Russell's *Boke of Nurture*. Apples, pears, nuts, caraways in comfit (i.e. in a sugar coating), and composts are mentioned elsewhere in the same book as suitable foods 'after meat . . . your stomach for to ease'.[4]

The composts were made from sliced root vegetables and pears mixed with raisins and currants, all preserved in a spiced syrup of sweet wine, honey, and vinegar, and they may have resembled a rather sweet chutney, for *The Forme of Cury*, the recipe-book compiled by the royal cooks about 1390, tells us that these ingredients were cast together in a pot of earthenware, 'and take thereof when thou wilt and serve forth'.[5] The spices, the composts, the nuts, and even the apples and pears, which were generally stored for some time before they were eaten, had one feature in common with the later 'banquetting stuffe': they were collected or, in the case of the confectionery and conserves, prepared well in advance of use. They were foodstuffs which could be kept for some time and brought out when the occasion demanded.

In the matter of the final course France once more led the way. In Paris in the 1390s, well-to-do middle-class families were already beginning to expand the final hippocras and wafers served after a grand dinner into a separate course of sweet dishes;[6] or even, in one example given by *Le Ménagier de Paris*, serving a separate course of sweet dishes and fruit called 'dessert' to precede the final hippocras and wafers. The dessert described by the *Ménagier* comprised compost with white and red spices scattered over it, perhaps in the form of sugared comfits; rissoles which were made from a spiced purée of apples and dried fruits formed into little balls and fried; flans; figs; dates; raisins; and hazelnuts. But for another occasion the dessert recommended by the same book was frumenty and venison, so it was not as yet fixed as a fully sweet course.[7]

Also from the *Ménagier*, we learn about the bourgeois equivalent of the *voidée*. After the hippocras and wafers comes the washing of hands, with a ewer and basin and a napkin brought round to each guest; then grace is said and the company, standing, partakes of wine and spices. In a very large establishment, the company withdraws to another room after grace and waits while the servants eat. Then the wine and spices are brought; and after that it is time to make one's *congé* and depart[8]. These glimpses from the *Ménagier* show two ideas which were to influence the development of the banquet: the separate dessert course; and the practice of withdrawing to another room for the final episode of the meal.

The course of sweetmeats which in France preceded the hippocras and wafers was eventually adopted in England; and in the fifteenth century the sweetmeats may even have been served alongside the hippocras and wafers, if John Russell's account is accurate. At the end of the fifteenth century, when the two final stages were made distinct as part of the concluding ritual of a very grand feast, we find that their relative order has already been reversed. As the feast for the enthronement of Archbishop Warham drew to a close in 1504, the Archbishop was solemnly served with hippocras and wafers; the surnappe (cloth) was removed from the board with great ceremony and show; his lordship washed his hands and said grace: 'And after this, standing at the voydée the said Lord Archbishop was served with comfits, sugar plate, fertes [sweet closed tarts], with other sotelties, with hippocras. And so departed to his chamber'.[9]

It was not so many years later that the separate banquet began to emerge, requiring the surprisingly wide range of sweetmeats which became known as 'banquetting stuffe'. **The fare of the Tudor banquet**

What exactly was 'banquetting stuffe'? The list of fare written down by Henry Machin in his diary entry describing the feast-day of the Skinners' Company on 10 June 1560 is tantalisingly brief: '... Master Clarenshaux made a great banquet for the Masters and the Company, first spiced bread, cherries, strawberries, pippins, and marmalade and sucket, comfits and portyngalles [semi-sweet oranges which took their name from Portugal] and divers other dishes, hippocras, Rhenish, claret wine and beer, and all great plenty and all was welcome'.[10]

It is a pity that his patience failed him by the time he reached 'divers other dishes'. But within a few years cookery-books were beginning to demonstrate the great variety of confections which might be served at the banquet course. Thomas Dawson listed the raw materials in *The Good Huswife's Iewell* of 1596 under the heading: 'The names of all things necessary for a banquet':

> Sugar, cinnamon, liquorice, pepper, nutmegs, all kinds of saffron, sanders, comfits, aniseeds, coriander, oranges, pomegranate seeds, Damask [rose] water, turnsole, lemons, prunes, [ordinary] rosewater, dates, currants, raisins, cherries conserved, barberries conserved, rye flour, ginger, sweet oranges, pepper white and brown, mace, wafers.[11]

Prominent on this list are the warming spices: cinnamon, nutmegs, mace, coriander, aniseeds, and pepper. Most of these spices had either been traditional flavourings for hippocras or had been served alone or sugar-coated at the final stage of a medieval feast. They had been valued partly in a post-prandial digestive role and partly for their flavours, for they sweetened the breath as well as settling the stomach. They were still popular for both reasons in Tudor and Stuart times, so they were included in most of the confections made up for the banquet.

But perhaps the most significant items on Thomas Dawson's list is the first one: sugar. The full repertoire of banqueting fare was enormous. Fresh locally grown fruits and imported dried fruits might be present. Virtually everything else had been mixed, cooked, baked, pounded, or otherwise worked or preserved with additions of sugar or, occasionally, honey. In many cases the proportion of sugar was high, and it not only supplied sweetness but also had a preservative function, thus permitting out-of-season fruits and flowers to be served at any time of year.

As well as the preserved fruits, flowers, and roots in their numerous different guises, and the fruit-flavoured stiff jellies and sugar pastes, there were the biscuit-breads, fine jumballs, and knots and other light cakey or biscuity confections; leaches, which were milk or cream jellies flavoured with almonds, spices and the ubiquitous rosewater and cut into slices for serving; sugar-candies, sugar-plate and spiced sugar-pastes variously shaped and coloured, and the sugar-covered spices known as comfits; also the marchpane, a handsome decorated marzipan confection which often took pride of place; sweet, dark gingerbread, made initially from breadcrumbs and spices, and only later mixed with flour and baked as a cake; and sweet, white almond-paste gingerbread gilded with leaf-gold. In the seventeenth century there were syllabubs, trifles, and other creamy dishes, and fresh cream cheese mixed with cream and flavoured with sugar, rosewater, and cinnamon. Interestingly, the cream-based confections do not appear in the earliest collections of recipes for 'banquetting stuffe'; they were added as cream went up in the world socially, having formerly been part of the peasant's 'white meats'.

To accompany the many and varied items of 'banquetting stuffe' there were sweet Southern European wines, as well as the traditional spiced hippocras; and there were also some of the newly fashionable 'hot waters', that is spirits of wine distilled over herbs, spices, and fruits, formerly medicines but now becoming part of the repertoire for social drinking. When used for that purpose, the distilled 'waters' were nearly always sweetened with sugar.

Sugar through the centuries Today sugar addiction is recognised as a health hazard. But not everyone realises that the ever-rising sugar consumption in Britain over the last three or four hundred years follows a much longer period when sugar was regarded as a beneficial medicine. Sugar had been known in southern Europe since the days of Alexander the Great. Yet the Romans apparently never recognised it as a sweetener for food, but only as a medicine. They imported small quantities from India and Arabia, and Dioscorides in the second century AD advised dissolving it in water and taking it in the form of a drink; he said it was good for the stomach, the bowels, the kidneys, and the bladder.[12]

It was probably the Persians who first adopted sugar as a foodstuff since they were growing the canes within their territories in the fifth and sixth centuries AD. At any rate, sugar is known to have been an ingredient in the cuisine of the later Abassid court, which looked back to Persian culture in other respects and may have done so also in the matter of sugar usage. Our earliest glimpses of sugar as a foodstuff, taken from Arab literary texts and the *Baghdad Cookery Book*, show it mixed with ground almonds, rolled up in strips of thin bread, cut into small slices, and soaked in a rosewater and sugar syrup; this confection was called 'lozenge'.[13] Rather more prosaically, sugar was scattered over cooked white rice. Yet even this was a fit subject for a court poet who compared the rice to snow and to the whitest milk: 'While sugar sprinkled upon every side/Flashes and gleams like light personified'.[14]

The sugar and ground almond mixture was one that came to the West at the time of the Crusades, no doubt through the influence of the Frankish Crusader kingdoms which survived at the eastern end of the Mediterranean for nearly two hundred years. But many other sugar usages reached Western Europe through Arab medical sources. Sugar continued to be valued in its medicinal aspect for centuries, and instructions for preserving fruits in sugar syrups and making other syrups from fruit juices appeared not just in cookery books but also in Arab medicinal and pharmaceutical handbooks. The various flowers, herbs, roots and seeds which were also preserved all had medicinal virtues of their own, and when they were conserved in this manner they took on the additional warming virtues of the sugar.

The Arabs planted sugar-canes on most of the larger Mediterranean islands which they occupied, and in their north African domains. By the later Middle Ages sugar had begun to arrive by way of trade in north-western Europe. Sugar came to England on the spice ships from Venice or Genoa, though its place of origin was further south. The medicinal connection persisted. Sugar was popular in medicine, being considered warm in the first degree and, therefore, more temperately heating than honey, which was warm in the second degree. It was still helpful to the stomach, and a cure for cold diseases, agues, and lung complaints. So, in the medieval West, the instructions for conserving flowers with sugar, and for making aniseed or caraway comfits and spiced sugar pastes, tended to be copied into collections of medical recipes (many of which also derived from the books of Arab physicians) rather than into cookery manuscripts.[15] The latter show only the direct use of sugar as a culinary sweetener, for instance in certain pottages and pies.

By the fifteenth century, recipes for chardequynce were beginning to appear occasionally in cookery-books, transferred there from the medical manuals. Chardequynce was the name given to a rather solid confection of spiced and jellied quinces, originally prepared with honey, but that was now being ousted gradually by sugar. John Russell said it was 'like to' the composts of pears and root vegetables in sweet–sour syrup in that it was to be taken at the end of a meal 'your stomach for to ease'.[16] Late medieval menus list such dishes as pears in syrup and dates in compost in the last course, alongside various meat or fish dishes; but it is possible that diners were already beginning to select these sweeter dishes to eat last of all out of the mixed array of foods set forth upon the board.

The use of spices As has been hinted already, spices resembled sugar in having a double role in the medieval domestic economy. They made food more palatable and helped to preserve it; and they all had specific medicinal powers, hence they were incorporated into pills and potions for the sick.

There was also a close correspondence in the way sugar and spices were treated before use. Sugar arrived at English ports on the spice ships, and in the large and wealthy households for which it was purchased it was charged to the spice account. Within a great house, it was stored alongside the spices and kept locked up, to be issued to the cook in relatively small quantities at a time.

This close conjunction between sugar and spices, which can be traced back to Arab medicine and Arab confectionery, continued in Britain all through the Middle Ages. During that time, some of the apparently 'medicinal' items were given roles in the realm of *social* eating. Social is the operative word here, for they were introduced into the special fare offered at great feasts to impress important guests, rather than into everyday foodstuffs.

Aniseed and caraway seed comfits covered with sugar were good for the digestion. But if some of the sugar they were dipped in was coloured red with sanders and turnsole, and some of it was left white, then the comfits were pretty enough to appear at a feast; so they were strewn on thick pottages as decoration, with contrasts achieved by putting white comfits on red or dark-coloured pottages, and red comfits on white ones. The comfits were to go on to become part of 'banquetting stuffe', where they became adornments for the marchpanes, or were served on their own as sweetmeats.

Penidia, or little tails, was the Latin name for another **Sweets and** confection, known in English as 'penides'. To make them, **pastes** sugar was boiled up with a little water and then drawn out into a long, narrow roll with an iron hook, and from the roll were cut small pieces 'as mychel as a small ynche'; they probably resembled modern barley-sugar sweets, and they were taken as a cure for colds. Yet even they were used sometimes to decorate medieval pottages.[17] But they, in contrast to the comfits, never really threw off their medicinal role; and although they do sometimes appear in Tudor and Stuart handbooks of 'banquetting stuffe' recipes, with their name shortened to 'pennet', they are always designated as being good for colds.

Various forms of spiced sugar-paste, such as paste royal, flavoured with ginger and mace and made more supple by an addition of honey; spiced almond paste; and chardequynce, the spiced quince jelly-paste, appear in medieval collections of sugar-work recipes. Although they, too, had medicinal connections — chardequynce was a digestive — they played an important part in the great feasts of the late Middle Ages, for they were the materials of the sotelties, the little scenes made up of human or animal figures which were carried in and displayed at the end of each course. Similar figures and devices decorated special dishes like the flampeyn (a large covered tart with pastry points) served in the middle course at the coronation feast of Henry V, which was flourished with the royal escutcheon, 'and therein three crowns of gold planted with fleurs de lis and flowers of enamel wrought of confections'.[18] The coloured sugar-flowers clearly glowed so brightly that they recalled the enamelled jewellery of the day.

The sugar-paste figures and objects had become very

complex by the end of the fifteenth century. This was
made possible by the introduction of gum tragacanth, the
resin from a shrub of Eastern Mediterranean origin, which
helped to bond and strengthen the paste. At first it was
used for simple objects, such as a 'sponge of sugar' made
by boiling gum tragacanth and other resins in white wine,
and reboiling the mixture with sugar and spices.[19] Then it
was added to the sugar-paste figures, which became ever
more elaborate. The sotelties usually expressed a serious
religious or allegorical theme, and the figures often bore
mottoes to explain their intent.

But the sugar-pastes of which the sotelties were made
had such possibilities that they could not fail to be taken
over as conceits for the banquet, though the figures
themselves took on homelier aspects. In the translated
Secretes of Alexis of Piedmont of 1562 is a recipe entitled,
'To make a paste of sugar whereof a man may make all
manner of fruits and other fine things with their form, as
platters, glasses, cups and suchlike things, wherewith you
may furnish a table, and when you have done, eat them
up. A pleasant thing for them that sit at the table.'[20] The
recipe carried just one warning about the sugar and gum
tragacanth paste: 'take heed there stand no hot thing nigh
unto it'. With the coming of the sotelties and decorated
marchpanes of the fifteenth century, sugar work was well
and truly parted from its medicinal origins, even though
the recipes were still being recopied into medical
handbooks. But the making of confectionery was not
taken over into everyday cookery. It was kept as a separate
activity, a state of affairs which was to continue into the
arrangements for making 'banquetting stuffe'.

The separation existed at the highest level. In the Royal
Household in the reign of King Edward IV there was an
Office of Greate Spycery, and on its staff was one clerk
whose duty it was to account for all spices and sugar: 'and
he to answer to every parcel of them in the
counting-house, as for sugar to the wafery, or to the sellar

or kitchen, with all other manner of spices needful to the confectionery and sawcery'. An Office of Confectionery also existed, where the sergeant 'receiveth of the Office of Greate Spycery all such stuff by indenture: all manner of spices to make confections, chardequynces, plates [i.e. spiced sugar-plate], seeds [i.e. the spices to be coated in sugar as comfits], and all other spicery needful; dates, figs, raisins great and small for the King's mouth and for his household in Lent season; wardens, pears, apples, quinces, cherries and all other fruits after season belonging to this office'.[21] Thus, a number of items which were later to form a significant part of 'banquetting stuffe' were already being gathered together and either prepared or manufactured in the Office of Confectionery at the late medieval court.

A further group of sweetmeats for the banquet, which again originated with the Arabs, remained medicinal for rather longer than the sugar and spice confectionery. It comprised the conserves made with citrus fruits. Bitter oranges, lemons, and pomegranates were first shipped to England from Spain in the thirteenth century, and within a few decades they too began to be brought in on the Italian ships. But it was not only the fruits themselves that arrived. Pots containing orange-peel or lemon-peel, or sometimes the whole fruits, conserved in sugar-syrup were another new import from Southern Europe. 'Succade' was the name given to this type of conserve, though occasionally it was called after the fruit it contained, as in the seven jars of 'sitrenade' brought into London on an Italian galley in 1420 along with a shipment of oranges and lemons.[22] As for their medicinal property, this was later summed up by Andrew Boorde, the physician: 'Oranges doth make a man to have a good appetite, and so do the rinds if they be in succade.'[23] Oranges and lemons arrived in greater numbers during the fifteenth century, but were still relatively costly. So, when these luxury fruits

Fruit
conserves

were purchased for a household, the juice went into sauces or pottages, but the lady of the house saved the peels and made her own succade from them, using either a honey syrup or one made from imported sugar. The method was to boil the peels in several changes of water to take off some of their bitterness, and then to give them a final boil in the sweet syrup in which they were to be stored.

In England this preserving technique was soon extended to health-giving herbs and roots, especially those which, like the sugar in the syrup, were helpful to the stomach and promoted good digestion, for example the roots and stems of angelica. John Gerard claimed for angelica that: 'it is a most singular medicine against surfeiting and loathsomeness to meat [meaning not merely fleshmeat, but all foodstuffs]; it helpeth concoction in the stomach, and is right beneficial to the heart'.[24]

In colloquial English, the succades of citrus peels and other fruit and vegetable conserves were called 'wet sucket' when they were kept in their syrup, and 'sucket candy' when they were dried out. But such medicines were too delicious to be reserved only for people suffering from nausea or surfeit. Just as the medieval composts, sliced pears, and root vegetables in a sweet–sour syrup were eaten at the end of a feast, so both wet and dry sucket were deemed appropriate for the conclusion of a meal and, once the banquet had been established, they easily took their place among the 'banquetting stuffe'.

In lists of goodies for the banquet, *marmalade* and succade are often named together, perhaps because the original imported versions so often arrived together on the same ships. Marmalade itself was a new luxury from Portugal which began to reach England in the fifteenth century; by 1495 Portuguese *marmelada* was arriving on Portuguese ships in sufficient quantities to be worth assessing for customs duty.[25] Its provenance is not surprising, since *marmelo* is the Portuguese word for the quince, from which *marmelada* was made. Its immediate predecessors were the spiced chardequynces and condoignacs of medieval Europe. The new feature which made it more interesting to northern Europeans than the familiar spiced quince jelly was its flavourings. For in *marmelada* the spices had been replaced by scents: rosewater and a little musk or ambergris. These again went back several hundred years as condiments in Arab cuisine, and they had long ago been adopted and put to work in a similar context in Spain and Portugal; but they were still quite a novelty in England. The first known English printed recipe for quince *marmelada* appeared in 1562 in the translated *Secretes* of Alexis of Piedmont. Possibly some earlier hand-copied recipes will eventually come to light in English manuscripts.

The discovery of the sugar/fruit-acid/heat bond, which produces pectin and is the basis of all fruit marmalades, jams, and jellies, was made in Roman times, when it was recognised only in the case of the pectin-rich quinces, but was never applied to other fruits. The reason was that the Romans liked to preserve fine fresh apples, peaches, plums, and other such fruits by submerging them in honey to exclude the air. But quinces, which are often still hard when picked, posed a problem because if they went into the honey hard, then they came out still harder. So quinces were precooked in wine, honey was added, and at that point the jelling pectin was released to set the quinces into a preserve. This was turned into a medicinal preparation very early on. Galen was said to have been the inventor of one form of it which used the juice only of the quinces, seasoned with ginger and white pepper, and his recipe became well known in Byzantine Greek medicine as a cure both for poor appetite and indigestion. From this and similar quince conserves the medieval chardequynce evolved.[26]

Yet for centuries there was apparently no attempt in

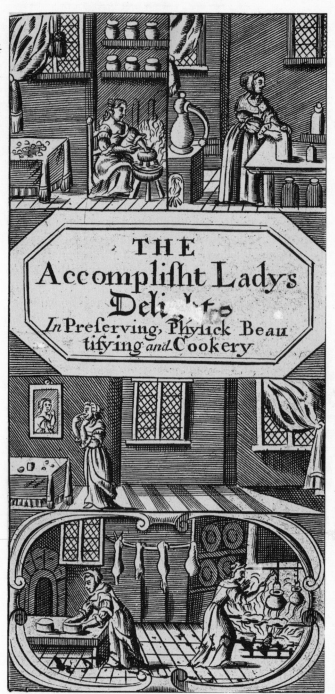

2.
Engraved title-page of
H. Woolley,
*The Accomlisht Ladys
Delight*, 1686.
The two pictures
above the title show
candying and
distilling.

THE
Accomplisht Ladys
Deli ｜·+o
In Preserving, Phyſick Beau
tifying *and* Cookery

north-western Europe to preserve other fruits by boiling them with honey, thus causing them to jell. Fruit was generally held in low esteem by the medical men of that region during the Middle Ages, and as late as 1541 Sir Thomas Elyot wrote: 'All fruits generally are noyful to man, and do engender ill humours, and be oft times the cause of putrefied fevers, if they be much and continually eaten.'[27] There was thus little desire to expend valuable honey or sugar on preserving such unsatisfactory forms of foodstuff. Only the Spanish and Portuguese, once again under Arab influence, carried out this type of preservation.

But in the sixteenth century the Italians, too, had come to recognise how delicious such conserves could be; and Alexis of Piedmont concluded his recipe for quince marmalade by pointing out that peaches and pears could be 'dressed...in like manner'. He also divulged the secrets of how cherries could be preserved whole with sugar, and peaches preserved in slices 'in the Spanish fashion.'[28] So the way was open for preserves of every kind of fruit to join the 'banquetting stuffe'. The early marmalades were all very solid, as Portuguese *marmelada* is to this day, to be cut with a knife and served out in slices. Orange marmalade, which also came from Portugal, was made by pounding the pectin-rich peel in a mortar along with the pulp and adding the whole mass to the juice. It set, after sugar had been put to it, into a thick, clouded jelly.[29]

Distilled 'waters', biscuits, syllabubs and fresh cheese

One further group of items which appeared at the banquet had a medicinal background, and that was the spice-flavoured distilled 'waters'. Home-distilling was practised in few but the greatest houses until after it had finally ceased to be practised in the monasteries in 1539. Thereafter, the small gentry and others began to equip stillrooms and stillhouses, primarily so as to be able to distil medical remedies at home. These included the alcoholic waters, distilled over herbs and spices, and also several non-alcoholic flower waters and, above all, rosewater, of which vast quantities were prepared in the rose season. (Orangeflower water, which became a fashionable flavouring in the seventeenth century, had to be imported from Southern Europe.) Rosewater had some medicinal uses: roses were cool in the first degree so rosewater was helpful in fevers. But its culinary importance was such that in many households most of the output must have gone into cakes, biscuits, leaches, jellies, fresh cream cheese and marchpanes. it was also a base for sweet-smelling scents for personal adornment. So it was present at the banquet in many different guises.

Alcoholic waters, distilled from wine over spices and sweetened with sugar, were there simply because they appeared to resemble the traditional spiced hippocras, but in a more concentrated form which induced feelings of well-being at a faster rate. Others began as medicines, like distilled clary water, good for back pain, but also noted for its aphrodisiac properties, which may be why it was eventually described as 'very wholesome, and fine entertaining water'.[30]

Small cakes and biscuits of several different types joined the wafers which had formerly been served along with hippocras to mark the end of the medieval meal. They fell into two main types: the light, dry biscuits, biscuit-breads and diet-breads; and the richer short cakes, for which the paste was mixed with butter or cream. The sweetened biscuit-breads show signs of being Italian by origin. The earliest English printed recipe to add this type of fare to the other sweetmeats is again among the *Secretes* of Alexis of Piedmont, and had the following curious title: 'To make little morsels, as they use in Naples, an exquisite thing for they be very savorous, do comfort the stomach and make a sweet breath.'[31] Since they comforted the stomach, they were clearly destined for the end of the meal, along with the 'banquetting stuffe'. The ingredients were sugar, flour, a little honey, and several spices; the liquid component was rosewater, and the paste was made up in the form of fishes.

In English recipe books, Alexis's 'little morsels' were developed under the name 'biskatello', and there was also a version called 'French bisket' which may likewise have had an ultimate Italian origin, for French Court cuisine came under Italian influence after Catherine de Medici married the French dauphin in 1533.[32] Another version of this sweetmeat which reached England from France was the almond macaroon, again with Italian overtones since the name is related to Italian *'macaroni'*.

In England, many forms of bisket and bisket-bread or diet-bread joined the 'banquetting stuffe'. Some were lightened with eggs and their recipes can resemble a modern sponge mixture; but long, slow cooking in the bread oven dried them out and brought their texture nearer to that of a sponge biscuit than to today's sponge-cake. Other sweet biscuit-breads were raised with ale-yeast, and they were usually well spiced with aniseeds, caraway- or coriander-seeds. They were made up into large rolls which were sliced and re-dried, in the manner of medieval biscuit; or into individual small rolls, which were often returned to a cool oven to dry out when they had already been cooked and cooled: 'So may you keep them half a year or longer; and if they chance through moist standing or weather to wax soft, give them a drying for an hour in an oven.'[33]

Jumballs or knots, little shaped or interlaced cakes, were made with pastes varying from the simpler 'bisket' type to those enriched with butter and ground almonds. Other small cakes were called 'fine cakes', or sometimes 'short cakes', and they contained butter or cream as well as eggs. They were made up small and baked on papers. The butter suggests an origin in Northern Europe rather than in the South, and they may have begun as a variant of 'puff', alias 'French puff', which was a piece of rich pastry, made in much the same way as today's butter puff pastry, and eaten by itself with sugar sprinkled over it.

The Elizabethan syllabub, which joined the 'banquetting stuffe', also reflected the Northern European dairying tradition, as did the fresh cream cheese flavoured with rosewater and cinnamon. Cream itself had long been associated with the dairy products eaten by medieval peasants and known collectively as 'white meats'. The idea thus grew up that the country folk of England had their own version of the banquet, based upon local fruits and cream. Andrew Boorde wrote, as early as 1542, that 'Raw cream, undecocted, eaten with strawberries or whortleberries is a rural man's banquet', adding darkly, 'I have known such banquets have put men in jeopardy of their lives'.[34]

Michael Drayton in a poem published in 1619 pictured shepherdesses and their swains settling down on the greensward to 'country cates', which were:

New whig, with water from the clearest stream,
Green plums and wildings, cherries, chief of feast,
Fresh cheese and dowsets, curds and clowted cream,
Spiced syllabubs and cider of the best.[35]

This pastoral aspect of 'banquetting stuffe' perhaps owes something to the outdoor element in the serving of the banquet, for in summer that ultimate course of the meal often took place in a garden banqueting house or summer house.

Traditional sweet fare There is one more group of dishes at the banquet to be set in context, and it is a mixed one, for it comprises several items already well established in fifteenth-century festal cuisine. They were served in the final main course, which was usually either the second or third course, where no more than two or three totally sweet dishes were laid out on the board in the company of a much larger number of meat or fish dishes. Their names can be read in the menus: pears in syrup; dates in compost; dates in comfit; leach

Lumbard (a thick paste of dates mixed with breadcrumbs and tempered with cream on a meat-day and almond milk on a fish-day); leach, coloured or white (either an enriched solid egg and milk custard, sliced, or, according to one recipe, already an almond milk and calf's foot jelly, foreshadowing the development of the Elizabethan white leach); payne puff, which is likely to have been a round of tender pastry similar to the later French puff (though the only recipe, which is in the *Forme of Cury,* is ambiguous, as it refers to the type of paste used in the previous recipe for sweet pastries);[36] gingerbread of breadcrumbs and spices incorporated with honey; doucettes and dariols (both forms of custard tart). All of these were adopted as they stood, or with some slight adaptations, into the fare of the banquet.

Jelly was sometimes a last-course dish, but was often still unsweetened, being either fish-based or jelled with swine or calf's foot, well-spiced, and set with pieces of fish or meat. But one fifteenth-century recipe shows the jelly already clear of meat and fish pieces, sweetened with sugar or honey, and with the option of purple, red, or yellow colourings, and this type of jelly went on to join the 'banquetting stuffe'.[37] Also to be found in the last course of a fifteenth-century feast was the marchpane. The marchpane at the coronation feast of King Henry V was 'garnished with divers figures of angels, among the which was set an image of St Katherine', obviously a compliment to Henry's queen, Katherine.[38] The marchpane, iced, gilded, patterned with coloured comfits and other sugar work, was to have pride of place among the 'banquetting stuffe'.

And who were the makers and consumers of all the delicious fare of the banquet? It was not confined to the great and noble households; it was copied more and more in the families of the small gentry and the successful yeomen farmers, and of the growing merchant class, who,

Sugar in 'banquetting stuffe'

during the sixteenth century, could afford to buy the necessary sugar, almonds and spices at the grocers' shops which, in turn, were increasing in number to meet the new demand.[39] Indeed, people could purchase many of the finished articles ready-made at the comfit-makers', if they so chose. But the country gentry grew their own fruits and herbs, and the townspeople could obtain theirs from the markets, supplied by the market-gardeners, another expanding trade. Then, as now, it was a matter of pride to one's self and it flattered one's friends if one offered them fare that was both attractive and *home-made*; and so a great deal of 'banquetting stuffe' was prepared at home.

Sugar was the catalyst in all this. In the earlier years of the sixteenth century its price had dropped to 3d or 4d per pound, which meant that, according to the money values of the time, it became a more affordable luxury. The cost of sugar was to fluctuate during the century. It rose to 9d or 10d per pound a few years before 1544, when its price inflation had to be checked by a royal proclamation.[40] It rose again towards the end of the century, when all food prices were inflated. But more and more sugar was coming onto the European market as supplies from the old sources — Crete, Sicily, and North Africa — were supplemented by sugar from the newer Portuguese and Spanish colonies on the Atlantic islands and in the New World.

Britain had no sugar colonies before 1616 when the canes were first planted in the Bermudas, so most of the sugar that entered the country came in by way of trade. It may be asked whether sugar brought in by the privateers, who harried the Portuguese and Spanish treasureships, provided any great addition. Robert Renger, a Southampton merchant, made the earliest recorded capture of sugar on a Spanish vessel, the *San Salvador*, in 1545. He took 124 chests of it, along with more valuable cargo in the form of gold, silver and pearls; and he is thought to have used up at least part of his sugar as gifts to people in high places at Court.[41] Sugar was a favourite gift — and bribe — of the period, although these gifts probably did little to spread its consumption more widely, and the privateers' sugar may not often have reached the open market.

As more and more of the sugar purchased for family use among the well-to-do was diverted into 'banquetting stuffe', so a new trend emerged. Because sugar needed special treatment when it was made into confectionery, sugar-working was outside the range of the average cook's experience. And, because it was still relatively costly, the lady of the house was not happy to hand over the work of converting it into 'banquetting stuffe' to her cook. So it was she, and her daughters and her maids, who gathered the flowers, fruits and seeds, candied and preserved them, and boiled up the sugar to make the syrups, comfits, and spiced sugar-plate.

Preparing 'banquetting stuffe'

And there was a further reason why the lady of the house took on this task. Sugar confectionery retained its medicinal importance alongside its role as the sweetener and preserver for luxury footstuffs. She was the wife of the head of the houshold, or perhaps head of the household in her own right. It was the duty of the woman in that position to look after the health of the other members of the household, and to supply medication for their minor ailments. If she was a kindly woman she did the same for poor neighbours and tenants.

Sugar and sugary conserves contributed to her supply of medicines. It is clear from apothecaries' accounts of Tudor and Stuart times that Manus Christi (sugar-work with gold leaf), sugar-candy, orange marmalade, aniseed and fennel-seed comfits, *diacitonium* (jellied quince with spices) and many other items of confectionery were prescribed as physic for the treatment of coughs, lung complaints, or stomach troubles.[42] Even biscuit-bread was made for physical (i.e. medicinal) use.[43] So the lady of the house liked to keep a supply of some of these things against unexpected illness, as well as for unexpected guests, just as she kept healing herbs and spices ready to hand to use for potions and plasters.

She also supervised the home-distilling of both simple and composite 'waters', drawn over many different herbs and spices, and of the great quantities of rosewater prepared for the household, though no doubt a manservant looked after the furnace and coped with the distilling apparatus. Because the stillroom or stillhouse was periodically warmed by the furnace, it was often chosen as a storeplace for 'banquetting stuffe', on the grounds that this would keep better in warm, dry air. In some cases the confectionery was actually made in the stillroom. Here the furnace could serve for the slow boiling of citrus peels, angelica stalks and suchlike for wet sucket and sucket candy. The furnace could also heat the portable stove, which was a sort of open iron cupboard with shallow shelves of copper-wire mesh, where sticky confections were dried out.[44] But the more delicate forms of sugar-work were carried out by the mistress and her maids over a chafing dish heated by charcoal, set upon a table. Leaches could be prepared over the chafing dish, too, though jelly-making probably continued to be kitchen work.

Some other forms of 'banquetting stuffe' also had to be made elsewhere: biscuit-bread and small cakes to be baked in the bread-oven, and the marchpane to have its icing set there, after it had been spread with 'an ice made of rosewater and sugar as thick as batter, spread it on with a Brush of Bristles, or with feathers';[45] fresh cream cheese and syllabubs to be produced in the dairy. In each case, the lady of the house supervised the arrangements, and it was to her that the printed collections of recipes were addressed.

And the consumers of the 'banquetting stuffe' were, of course, the same lady and her family, and their relatives and friends. The banquet, like many other social institutions, began at the highest level, at Court and in great noble households; and since members of the lesser gentry were sometimes invited, it soon filtered down as a new fashion for their families, and thence to the families of the well-to-do merchants and yeomen farmers. Tea-drinking made a similar progress down the social scale after it had been introduced at Court by Catherine of Braganza, wife of King Charles II. But whereas tea could be sold in very small amounts and was also counterfeited from the leaves of local trees, so that it ultimately reached the poorest and lowliest people, 'banquetting stuffe' did not penetrate so far. Sugar remained relatively costly, and honey which could sometimes be a substitute was never a cheap foodstuff. So the banquet in its full glory progressed only a certain distance through the ranks of English society.

The early recipe books for 'banquetting stuffe' reflect its original social milieu in titles like *Delightes for Ladies* and *A Closet for Ladies and Gentlewomen*. But Gervase Markham, himself a member of an old gentry family in Nottinghamshire, recognised well enough that the social setting of the banquet was being extended. When, in *The English Huswife* of 1615, he not only tells his 'huswife' how to make her 'banquetting stuffe' but also follows up the recipes with special instructions as to the order in which each kind of sweetmeat is to be carried in and laid out, 'no two dishes of one kind going or standing together, and this will not only appear delicate to the eye, but invite the appetite with the much variety thereof', then we know that the banquet has arrived as a national institution not only for the gentry, but also for the folk of the middling sort.[46]

Notes

1. *Oxford English Dictionary*
2. Walter of Bibbesworth, in *Curye on Inglysch*, ed. C. B. Hieatt and S. Butler (Early English Text Society, SS 8, 1985), p.3.
3. For a very formal example of the *voidée* and the regulations governing it as ordained in 1494 at the Court of King Henry

VII, see *A Collection of Ordinances and Regulations for the Government of the Royal Household*... (London: Society of Antiquaries, 1790), p.113.

4. J. Russell, *The Boke of Nurture*, ed. F. J. Furnivall (Early English Text Society, OS 32, 1868), pp.121–2.

5. *Forme of Cury*, in Hieatt and Butler, *Curye on Inglysch*, pp. 120–1, no. 103.

6. *Le Ménagier de Paris*, ed. G. E. Brereton and J. M. Ferrier (Oxford, 1981), p.175.

7. Ibid., pp.183–4.

8. Ibid., p.184.

9. R. Warner, *Antiquitates Culinariae* (London, 1791), p.115.

10. J. J. Lambert, *Records of the Skinners of London* (London, 1933), p.203.

11. T. Dawson, *The Good Huswife's Iewell* (1596, reprinted Amsterdam, 1977) C7v–C8.

12. Dioscorides, *Materia medica*, II. 82.4.

13. A. J. Arberry, 'A Baghdad Cookery Book', *Islamic Culture*, 13 (1939), pp.23, 211.

14. Ibid., p.27.

15. E. Brunskill, 'A Medieval Book of Herbs and Medicine', *Northwestern Naturalist*, n.s. 1 (1953–4), pp.181–6.

16. Russell, pp.121–2.

17. *Diversa cibaria*, in Hieatt and Butler, *Curye on Inglysche*, p.49, no. 33.

18. Warner, p. xxxvii.

19. Brunskill, p. 185.

20. Alexis of Piedmont (Girolamo Ruscelli), *The Secretes of the Reverend Maister Alexis of Piedmont* (London, 1562), ff.62v–63. For more on gum tragacanth, see J. Gerard *The Herball* (London, 1597), p.1149.

21. 'Liber niger', in *A Collection of Ordinances and Regulations*... (1790), p.81.

22. L. F. Salzman, *English Trade in the Middle Ages* (Oxford, 1931), p.414.

23. A. Boorde, *A Compendyous Regyment, or A Dyetary of Helth, 1542*, ed. F. J. Furnivall (Early English Text Society, ES 10, 1870), p.286.

24. J. Gerard, *The Herball* (London, 1597), pp. 847–8.

25. C. A. Wilson, *The Book of Marmalade*, (London, 1985), pp.30–2.

26. Ibid., p.22.

27. Sir Thomas Elyot, *The Castel of Helth ... augmented* (London, 1541), ff.23v–24.

28. Alexis of Piedmont, ff.62v, 64v, 62.

29. Sir Hugh Platt, *Delightes for Ladies* (London, 1605), A34.

30. E. Smith, *The Compleat Housewife* (London, 1727), pp.237–8.

31. Alexis of Piedmont, ff.64v–65.

32. Platt, A19–A21.

33. Lord Patrick Ruthven, *The Ladies Cabinet Enlarged and Opened*

(London, 1654), pp.32–3, no.72.

34. Boorde, p.267; cf. Russell, p.122, lines 81–4.
35. M. Drayton, *Poems*, ed. J. Buxton, vol. 1 (London, 1953), the 9th Eglogue, p.68.
36. For leach: ed. T. Austin, *Two Fifteenth-century Cookery Books*, (Early English Text Society, OS 91, 1888), p.37. no.17; for puff: Hieatt and Butler *Forme of Cury*, p.145, no.204.
37. Warner, p.61.
38. Ibid., p.xxxvii.
39. J. Youings, *Sixteenth-century England*, (Pelican History of Britain, 1984), pp.275, 290.
40. Ibid, p.144.
41. Ibid., pp.234–5.
42. The items quoted here are drawn from H. Bayles, 'Notes on Accounts paid to the Royal Apothecaries in 1546 and 1547', *Chemist and Druggist* (June 1931), p.796; and *Henry Power memoranda* (British Library, Ms Sloane 1351), f.69v = apothecary's accounts for December 1665.
43. Ruthven, p.33.
44. P. J. B. Le Grand d'Aussy, *La Vie Privée des Francoises d'Autrefois*, nouv. ed. (Paris, 1815), II, pp.317–8; R. Feild, *Irons in the Fire* (Marlborough, 1984), pp.204, 206, 247. The stove received many mentions in English seventeenth-century recipes.
45. Ruthven, p.26, no. 59.
46. G. Markham, *The English Huswife* 4th ed. (London, 1631), pp. 136–7.

3.

'Sweet Secrets' from Occasional Receipt to Specialised Books: The Growth of a Genre

LYNETTE HUNTER

Sugar and Spice and all things nice
that's what little girls are made of.

Soon after sugar began to be imported into England, its use developed a three-part history as medicine, preserving agent, and decoration.[1] From the thirteenth century onwards the aspects were often combined — sugared-fruits and sweetmeats were part of the delicacies offered at the end of the course or meal as a digestive — but in practice the three areas defined rather different uses of sugar. The emergence of 'banquetting stuffe' during the sixteenth century marks the beginning of an explicit separation between the three, and by the end of the seventeenth century medicinal uses of sugar were quite separate from domestic preserving skills and the emerging confectionery trade. This chapter will first look at the development of the word 'banquet' in the context of sugar, and will then assess three main periods of book publication relevant to the topic: 1575–84; 1602–17; and 1652–70.

The banquet 'Banquet' was a name which, in the 1530s, came to be used for foods that had been current for a considerable time. What prompted the changes was a complex series of events partly to do with the increased quantity of sugar entering England, partly to do with social changes, and partly to do with the introduction of the banqueting house[2] — a specific and different place for eating these increasingly specialised foods which made necessary a more discrete way of organising the recipes for them and a far more thorough description of their construction. Courses in medieval feasts had ended with a 'soteltie', which was part-pageant, part-entertainment, and often culinary. John Russell's *Boke of Nurture* (c. 1450) details the late medieval pattern of courses in which each ends with an increasingly large selection of sweet foods such as jellies, mawmaney, and comfits; more important, the final course consists solely of apples, sugar-candy, ginger, wafers, spiced cakes, and hippocras. It is this final course which yielded 'banquetting stuffe', although it is sometimes included along with the penultimate course of small fowl and sweetened foods. The foods in it had a digestive function. John Russell gives specific directions about which fruits are to be eaten before dinner and which after, and about which foods to avoid unless eaten with either hippocras or that other common digestive, cheese.[3] It is clear that many of the recipes were considered as medical secrets.

The word 'banquet' surfaces in direct relation to sweetmeats in the early 1530s in conjunction with the banqueting house,[4] and stays current until around 1700. Previously 'banquet' had been used for large festive meals, but between 1530 and 1700 the word 'feast' was often used for this purpose. 'Banquet' has now reverted to a large meal, but frequently with connotations of celebration, as in wedding banquet or the meal served at a ball, rather than the more ritual festive meals or feasts at Christmas and New Year. What is particularly intriguing is why the word 'banquet' should have taken over from the earlier 'soteltie'. Indeed the French used the earlier word for much longer—until the mid-seventeenth century, when both La Varenne and Lemery began to use 'sommelerie' instead.

This is possible because in France the medicinal value of these foods was emphasised for a longer period of time. During the sixteenth century in France, the word *'subtil'* applied both to the *aperitif* and the *attenuant,* although the *attenuants* specifically *'subtilient les grosses humeurs',* cleaned out viscousness and opened the passages. The *Conservation de Santé,* a 1572 translation of an earlier Latin medical work, also emphasises that *'subtils'* are digestive, not nourishing.[5] And even now a French rather than an English meal will include a 'digestif'.

Entangled in the English use of 'soteltie' is the idea of a skilled piece of craft work, as well as an interlude or *entremet* within a meal included for the purpose of entertainment, and specifically allied with the tradition of disguise or mumming that accompanied the pageants which interspersed the feasts of great occasions throughout the fourteenth to fifteenth centuries.[6] There is a curious cross between the pageant and the sugar-work aspects in an account of a feast given by the Duke of Burgundy in February 1454. The soteltie devised partly consisted of a huge pie within which were placed twenty-eight musicians; these struck up in response to the arrival of guests who entered following their meal in another room.[7] Although this element of pageant never completely deserted the soteltie, towards the sixteenth century the word came to refer more frequently to the magnificent sugar-work architecture created for the end of each course.

With the shift in place for eating foods at the turn of the fifteenth century, there came a shift in the role of sugar-works and sweetmeats. This also coincided with the publication in the vernacular of Plato's *Symposium,* not to mention those of Xenophon and Plutarch — *symposia* being banquets.[8] Dante's *Convivio,* also a 'banquet', was printed a number of times in the late 1520s[9] and would probably have been known to those English educationists such as Thomas Elyot and later, Roger Ascham, for its

defence of the vernacular. Indeed, it was closely followed
by Elyot's *Banquet of Sapience* of wit, aphorism, and subtle
sayings: small delicate morsels to stimulate the mind, very
much allied with the earlier idea of a digestive.[10] The use
was appropriate not only to the foods of the banquet meal
but also to the idea of engaging after-dinner conversation,
in contrast to another word which appears at the same
time 'rere-supper'. A rere-supper seems to have been more
specifically for men alone, during which they simply
became very drunk. One was clearly supposed to function
coherently throughout a banquet. Even a century later J.
Starkey (1678) translates from the French a curious treatise
against gluttony,[11] inveighing against 'prologues of
breakfasts; interludes of banquets; epilogues of rere-
suppers', and notes the dramatic and literary associations
of the description. The qualities of wit and wisdom
associated with the literary banquet appear to
metamorphose 'sotil' into the more modern sense of
'subtle' through association with the sweetmeat course. In
England the role of banqueting food is not only
medicinal, but from the start specifically for pleasure and
entertainment, although none the less secret. As the
books reveal, the secrets of the table are as important to
social status as those of medicine to physical health.

The emergence of the banquet as a social event ran
concurrently with a number of other developments
pertinent to its growth and popularity. The early sixteenth
century saw the beginnings of the printed book in
England, an enormous scale of social and economic
change, as well as a growing specialisation of knowledge as
the arts and sciences separated and fragmented. Each of
these developments had substantial bearing on the way in
which 'banquetting stuffe' was portrayed in the media.

   With the invention of moveable type during the late
fifteenth century, and the inauguration of Caxton's press,
books in England became increasingly available, if

The emergence of cookery-books

expensive and restricted to standard works. It was, however, unusual to have the considerable amount of vernacular printing that Caxton encouraged, a trend quite unlike the continental practice from which England was isolated. Even so, there were relatively few books relating to cookery until the latter part of the sixteenth century. Not only was it a less respectable written form, having been denigrated from Plato onwards, but also people did not need cookery-books. Those who had to cook knew how to do so, having learnt from oral tradition. Not that cookery- books are simply to do with recording past recipes and teaching new ones — they are part of a far more complex picture of changing supplies in foodstuffs, publishing history, and the shifting social, political, and economic structures. But in contrast to everyday cookery, the kinds of food made for banquets were not only part of a recognised tradition in medical literature but their preparation was not widely practised. They would have been made by cooks in large aristocratic households; yet with increasing supplies of sugar and an increasing moneyed class emulating the aristocratic social events, more people needed to know how to make these foods. There was a need for books to help them do so, and the gentry were precisely the people who could afford books. Indeed, the result of these factors is that sugar-work and sweetmeats made up the earliest printed cookery-books in the English language.

By the mid-sixteenth century, if not considerably earlier,[12] the housewife of the gentry was expected to know some basic uses of sugar-cookery as part of her medicinal knowledge. For example, Thomas Tusser's *One Hundreth Pointes of Good Husbandrie/Huswiferie* (1557) mentions conserves of barbarie and quince, as well as syrups. And this work, a classic early version of the city–country critique, was intended for the country housewife, not just the fashionable urban gentry. But the first substantial introduction to these foods was the translation into

English of Alexis of Piedmont's *Secretes,* by W. Warde in 1558. This work had originally been written in Latin, and had established a pattern for the transmission of medical receipts followed by many subsequent writers. *Secretes* consists of general remedies, perfumes, sugar-work, including the use of honey and the making of lozenges, pastes, confections, and comfits, and concludes with household receipts and general alchemical science. The book treats sugar-work in the same way as almost all books up to this time, entirely in terms of medicine, and these were indeed medical secrets.

The book which broke the pattern and established a radically new treatment for cookery receipts was John Partridge's *The Treasurie of Commodious Conceits and Hidden Secrets* (1573). The title continues:

The Housewives Closet of Healthful Provision. Mete and necessarie for the profitable use of all estates both men and women: and also pleasant to recreation ... Gathered out of sundrye experiments lately practised by men of great knowledge.

The vocabulary summarises the early Elizabethan period. There is treasurie and profit, for use and for pleasure, hidden secrets but also sundry experiments; there is the housewives' closet versus the knowledge of great men, but also the receipts are for all men and women of all estates. The words provide a fascinating vision of the future Elizabethan and Jacobean world. A world of commerce, of the emerging middle class; a world which splits the factual from the emotional, calling into question the whole basis of value. A world moving men from the secrets of alchemy to the open experiments of science — although it should be noted that one of the benefits of experimental science was supposed to be its private nature[13] — from God's world to humanism and nature. At the same time this world left women with the closet, the closed door on their lives which were filled with events unknown to men, and therefore to be feared; the closet was a world which was neither God's nor man's, and therefore easily filled with the unnatural secrets of witchcraft. Yet, in 1573, the vision is more balanced, both with men and women, and all estates caught up into this shifting world.

Partridge's *Treasurie* was one of the most influential and long-running books of the period, being published fairly consistently until 1637. The work has many similarities with Master Alexis's *Secretes,* but places the emphasis firmly on the banquet. Beginning with a section on the cooking of small fowl which looks back to the penultimate course of the late medieval feast, the receipts then move into a substantial and representative section on marchpanes (marzipan), tarts, blaunch powder (sugar and spice), the use of quinces, condiates of fruit, conserves of roots and flowers, syrups, Manus Christi (sugar-work with gold leaf), lozenges and hippocras (spiced wine). The book only then moves on to receipts for medicines, perfumes, and household goods in general.

It is clear that Partridge is appealing to a very specific audience, and the extensive forematter indicates this aim. The book begins with a poem by the author which claims 'to Frame/A happy common weale:/And which at large reveals,/That tyme dyd long conceale,/To pleasure everyone'; in other words he is intending to disclose previously restricted secrets to a large public for purposes of pleasure and entertainment. He then goes on in the dedication to expand on the secret nature of these receipts. The dedication is to a Richard Ditton, assistant in the Guild of Barbers and Surgeons, which was established in 1540. In it Partridge speaks of providing receipts of 'hidden secrets' for foods such as conceits and marmalades that have 'not hitherto ben publiquely known'. He adds that he does this despite a possible backlash of jealousy from the rich who have assumed that 'farre fette and deare bought, is good for great Estates' and may now blacklist him or simply refuse to buy the book.

Such an assumption is, he suggests, similar to rejecting the attentions of physicians or surgeons simply because by their constitution into guilds (physicians in 1518) they have become more available to the public.

A significant but concealed undertone to the forematter is concerned with the other set of associated secrets: the culinary secrets of sugar-work were specific neither to the physicians nor to the surgeons, but to the apothecaries. Although not yet constituted as an effective guild, the apothecaries did attempt a form of protectionism over sugar-work, albeit not so tightly controlled as their counterparts in Germany, where the immensely popular products of sugar were almost exclusively bought from apothecaries.[14] Partridge is ensuring here that their skills are made public and available. The dual nature of the secrets as both medical and social is underlined by other poems to the author in the forematter: one noting his concern with revealing the secrets of medicine and another explicitly commenting on the secrets of food preparation. They make clear the curious elision from the disguise and ritual of mumming and pageant from the mystery of alchemy, to the private sign of guild or aristocratic class privilege. Possibly due to criticism, another book produced by John Partridge ten years later, *The Widowes Treasure* (1584), had far more emphasis on the general medicinal and far less on sweetmeats.

One of the earliest printed books of general cookery is A. W.'s *A Booke of Cookry* (1584), which includes sweetmeats as a subsection of tarts. This is unique in arrangement since it is the only subsection in the book. It appears that the writer recognises these foods as distinct, yet not normally included within cookery. The arrangement is significant since the book is otherwise divided in terms of specific, well-recognised constituents of the dinner-table, and thus provides a good indication of the more general use of sugar in cooking at this time. As one moves down the social scale to the emerging commercial classes, it is reasonable to suggest that there was less possibility for building separate rooms within which to eat these foods, so they may have incorporated them in the latter stages of a meal much as their fifteenth-century forebears. It is notable that in the next edition of *A Book of Cookrye* (1587), the only changes made to the book are in the additions of recipes to this section alone, indicating the growing demand for them — a demand recognised increasingly in books over the following fifteen to twenty years.

The next major period of importance to books relating to sugar-works starts in 1602 with the publication of the anonymous *Closet for Ladies and Gentlewomen*, which, along with Hugh Platt's *Delightes for Ladies* (1605)[15] received continuous publication for fifty to seventy years. Curiously, although these two works cover much of the same ground, they are often bound together. *Delightes* contains sections on preserves and conserves as well as candying, distillation, cookery, and beauty. The *Closet* covers preserves and conserves and 'banquetting stuffe', medicines and distillation. To bind together two such books implies that people wanted cookery from one, medicines from the other, and sugar-work and 'banquetting stuffe' from both. Indeed, one copy at the Brotherton Library binds together the cookery section from *Delightes* and sugar-work and medicine from the *Closet*, alone.

Despite the clear need for both, these two works are particularly interesting because they present the first real split between sugar-works as a household skill and as a medicinal skill. Even the titles, with the *Closet* as a place for secrets and cures and *Delightes* as a source of entertainment, underline this division. Hugh Platt's epistle specifically lays out his pleasurable intent:

By now my pen and paper are perfum'd,
I scorne to write with coppresse or with gall,

DELIGHTES
FOR LADIES, TO
adorne their Persons,
Tables, Closets, and
Distillatories:

With

BEAVTIES, BANQVETS,
Perfumes & Waters.

Reade, Practice, & Censure.

AT LONDON,
Printed by HVMFREY
LOWNES.
1609.

3.
Title-page from
Sir Hugh Platt,
Delightes for Ladies, 1611
edition.

Barbarian canes are now become my quills,
Rosewater is the ink I write withall:
Of sweetes the sweetest I will now commend,
To sweetest creatures that the earth doth beare: . . .
Let pearcing bullets turne to sugar bals,
The Spanish feare is husht and all their rage.

The corollary of the separation is that medicine is moving away from being a domestic skill, specifically part of the housewife's learning — a role it had occupied until at least 1577, when the duties of older women are defined as skill in surgery, distillation, and artificial practices.[16] The artificial is swiftly becoming unnatural and prohibited.

The *Closet's* section explicitly on sugar-work as 'banquetting stuffe' put a name to this growing area of cookery which was maintained by other books of the period. Enormously popular was Gervase Markham's *Country Contentements* (1615), which included the book *The English Huswife*, with a specific section of 'banquetting stuffe and conceited dishes'. However, even at this date, there is a confusion about 'banquetting stuffe' on the part of the compositors and printers which indicates the probability that these foods were restricted in consumption. Although the rest of the book is neatly set out with running headlines relating to each section, in 'banquetting stuffe' one finds the headlines 'cookery' or 'feasts' continually intruding. The entire section caused a classic bibliographic problem in pagination which was not sorted out until the 1688 edition.

In the part on 'banquetting stuffe' Markham gives instructions about a wide range of cooking, and also provides one of the few descriptions of how the foods should be served, indicating the relative novelty of such dishes to at least part of his audience. That audience was primarily the country gentry, but this well-written and fairly well-printed book found a much wider urban audience and began to reflect its consensus in later editions. The first edition notes that 'banquetting stuffe' is 'not of general use, yet ... whosoever is ignorant therein is lame, and but the half part of a compleat housewife', and goes on to explain that once the reader is 'exact and rehearsed in the rules' other housewifery 'secrets' can be introduced: those of distillation, waters, perfumes, incense, pomanders, vinegars, verjuice. Later editions displace these conceits into an awkward position towards the end of the book, and replace the material on 'banquetting stuffe' with a more urban and sophisticated concern: 'skill in the ordering of feasts'.

Nevertheless, *The English Huswife* is part of *Country Contentements*, which contains sections on domestic medicine, cookery, brewing, and so on, as well as 'banquetting stuffe', and definitely holds to the traditional role of the woman as skilled in all these areas. Significantly for a writer who provides in 1615 a substantial opening section on medicine, Markham notes in his 1616 revision of Charles Estienne's *The Country Farm* — a work directed towards male managers of large country farms — that while women do have the responsibility of looking after their family's health they should do so 'with sobrietie, not medling, above their place and reach, in matters of Physicke; and [with] Gravitie, as [like] not having anything to do in the matter of Fukes [hair fashions]' or they will lead a 'loose and very sinful life'. Why this rather surprising statement should be made may have to do with the impending incorporation of the Apothecaries' Guild (1617). It is not surprising that John Murrell's *A Daily Exercise for Ladies and Gentlewomen* (also 1617) advertises itself as a fashion book, comparing the newest strain of conserves with the recent fashionable change from blue to yellow ruffs,[17] although most of the recipes are quite ordinary repetitions from older works.

John Murrell's contribution was one of the last to be made until 1652, with the exception of Lord Patrick Ruthven's *The Ladies Cabinet*, published in 1639 and not

4.
An extract from
G. Markham,
The English Huswife,
1631 edition.

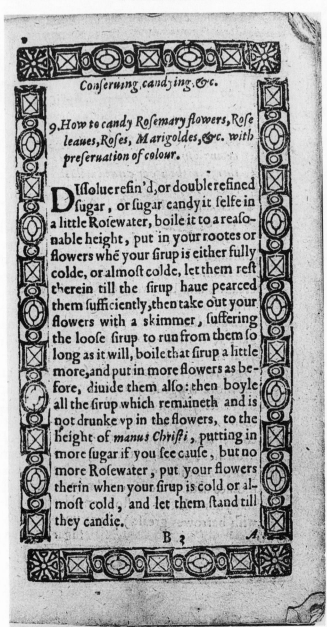

Conſeruing, candying. &c.

9. *How to candy Roſemary flowers, Roſe
leaues, Roſes, Marigoldes, &c. with
preſeruation of colour.*

Dissolue resin'd, or double refined
ſugar, or ſugar candy it ſelfe in
a little Roſewater, boile it to a reaſo-
nable height, put in your rootes or
flowers whē your ſirup is either fully
colde, or almoſt colde, let them reſt
therein till the ſirup haue pearced
them ſufficiently, then take out your
flowers with a skimmer, ſuffering
the looſe ſirup to run from them ſo
long as it will, boile that ſirup a little
more, and put in more flowers as before, diuide them alſo: then boyle
all the ſirup which remaineth and is
not drunke vp in the flowers, to the
height of *manus Chriſti*, putting in
more ſugar if you ſee cauſe, but no
more Roſewater, put your flowers
therin when your ſirup is cold or almoſt cold, and let them ſtand till
they candie.

B 3   A.

republished until 1654.[18] Ruthven recognises the implicit divisions in the publishing history of the *Closet* and *Delightes* by separating the recipes into preserves, medicines, and cookery. He notes in the forematter that medicines are the most important area; they are 'rare secrets' bounded on each side by 'delightes for pleasure, sport and pomp' (sugar-works) and by neat cooks. The book is still part of a serious explanatory study, although, in adapting to the new experimental procedures, Ruthven is caught up in their ambivalence. In practice, as the title suggests, its aim is to improve nature by art. Indeed, Ruthven extends the conflation of old and new analogies: he says he will lay each jewel, or item of knowledge, in its particular box, providing a *tabulation* for their cabinet, a *fixed* design and place for items in the mysterious world. From this period on, secrets are rarely other than medicinal, and sugar-work is neither medicinal or secret.

Ruthven's *The Ladies Cabinet* is an anomaly; however, it sets a pattern for the presentation of sugar-cookery, which was followed during the next main period for related books from 1652 to 1670. Why the hiatus in cookery and sugar-work books between 1617 and 1652 should have occurred is problematic. The incorporation of the Guild of Apothecaries in 1617 is clearly a contributing factor. In 1618 the following of the *London Pharmacopoeia* became mandatory for practising apothecaries.[19] The power of the guild increased dramatically until 1632, when its central hall was opened in London, and it remained powerful until at least 1640, when the events of the commonwealth began to shift the emphasis of government.[20] There is the possibility that the persecution of witches which came to a head under James I may have had some significance since the medical skills in question were increasingly viewed as unnatural if practised by women.[21] But there was further harassment in the early 1630s by Charles I. Many scores died in the purges of the 1640s and killing continued from 1650 to 1670 concurrent with the next upsurge in popularity for the books.

A more likely set of factors may have to do with the 1615 Star Chamber decrees restricting the printing of books to twenty master printers in London, Oxford and Cambridge. These printers were allowed only one or two presses, and there were limitations on the number of type-casters.[22] The rate of all printing was slowed down, particularly the popular and vernacular printing which was not going to be of an immediate profitable return, such as dramatic works. At the same time, stricter rules about copyright were instituted so that one could republish without re-entering the book for the Stationers' Register only as long as the copyright ownership remained the same: indeed Markham's *The English Huswife* remained within one firm throughout successive editions from the 1630s to the 1650s. However, reprints were not markedly reduced. It is the lack of any original works that is startling.

It may be that the works published to 1617 were adequate, the market saturated, and fashions stable. As cookery was being excluded from serious consideration, possibly their contents were not respectable enough to merit new work by the few people who could write them. It is the case that until this hiatus these books were by and large written by men, and that after 1652 they were increasingly written by women. Not only was this still a woman's province in practice, but it also became less associated with the pursuit of serious inquiry by interested gentlemen. The events of the commonwealth, particularly aspects of reformation religion, radically altered the education of the less-privileged majority of the population; and certainly shifted the whole structure of social expectation, particularly for women.[23] Also, supplies of food were changing. At the same time sugar was flooding into England in unprecedented quantities and was becoming available to a broader group of people.

Certainly, by the late 1670s, the use of sugar was widespread in urban cooking practices.

Oddly, one contributing factor to the re-emergence of these books after 1652 may have been the execution of Charles I in 1649. Most of the related works published during this later period, even during the 1650s and the latter years of the commonwealth, make specific reference either in their titles or their provenance to royalty or aristocracy — although it is clear that both Royalist and Roundhead enjoyed banquets. Elizabeth Cromwell certainly included 'banquetting stuffe' in large feasts ordered for special events such as the visit of the French Ambassador in 1656.[24] But while the scope of the books returns, the relevant recipes are rarely connected with the term 'banquetting stuffe'.

Among many other publications is that in 1653 by W. J., Gent. of *A Choice Manual of Rare and Select Secrets in Physick and Chirugery*, which includes preserves, bound in with *A True Gentlewoman's Delight*, which included cookery; both were attributed to the Countess of Kent.[25] The 1653 editions show that they have been printed separately but often bound together. Presumably they were conceived of as two separate books but put together by W. J., possibly because he was capitalising on the countess's name. What is interesting is that the *True Gentlewoman* is primarily about cookery, but with a sugar-work section advertised specifically as 'very necessary for all ladies and gentlewomen', as if the writer is aiming at a wider audience but noting that the gentrified reader will not be as concerned with cookery as with the gentle art of confectionery. The 1656 edition is already purportedly the ninth, and the work must have been popular even looking at the evidence of the large number of copies remaining today. The ninth edition prints both the *Choice Manual* and *True Gentlewoman* in one, deleting the candying and preserving section from the *Choice Manual,* and indicating the continued demand for all of the skills relating to medicine, cookery and sugar-work.

The two parts were published usually as one book until 1687, but even they are far outdone by *A Queen's Closet Opened, Incomparable ... Secrets* (1655), attributed to Queen Henrietta Maria, wife of Charles I, and brought together by a 'W. M.' Henrietta Maria died in 1669, but the work continued to be published until 1713. *A Queen's Closet* is made up of the *Pearl of Practice* (medicine), *A Queen's Delight or the Art of Preserving* (sugar-work), and the *Compleat Cook* (cookery), again maintaining that three-part division of Ruthven's *Ladies Cabinet*. But here the parts are clearly thought of as distinct and separate. One often finds just one section alone bound in what appears to be a unique edition. There are, for example, even at a rough estimate, twenty-one or twenty-two editions of *A Queen's Delight*, but only sixteen or so of *A Queen's Closet, Pearl of Practice*,[26] and each part changes according to the times. Early eighteenth-century editions of the three together advertise them as 'after the newest Modes'; but *A Queen's Delight* incorporates substantial changes during late seventeenth-century editions, particularly the inclusion of definitions for clarifying and boiling of sugar lifted directly from La Varenne's *Le Parfait Confiturier* (1668).

The practice of combining sugar-work, medicine, and cookery also continued into the 1670s and 1680s, but with increasing specialisation. The pattern of distinct and separate publication (but joint bindings) for *A Queen's Closet* was the precursor of a fashion which published specialist books more and more for career or vocational purposes, and combined the areas in a less rigorous manner for general domestic use. There are, of course, always exceptions, and Robert May's *Accomplish't Cook, or the Art and Mystery of Cooking* (1664) is an important example. The work is anomalous in several ways, possibly reflecting May's career as a cook to the aristocracy from the 1630s to the 1650s, having spent much time working in

France cooking for exiled families during the Commonwealth. Unlike many writers of the period, he includes most of his sugar-work recipes in a section on 'tarts for banquetting', explicitly using the word. One has to realise that during this period the English were renowned for their poor fruit preserves. Indeed, they were accused of over-boiling and disguising bad fruit with sugar. But the French had the treatment of fruit down to an art. Markham notes of English and French differences as early as the *Country Farm* (1616, p.2), that 'we are as farre from their fruits, as they from our wools'. Many English accounts of buying sweetmeats abroad are concerned with the purchase of fruit conserves,[27] but in terms of confectionery the English are highly skilled: the French looked on the English as a nation of sweet-eaters,[28] and the reputation was so widespread that later writers on confectionery sometimes felt the need to defend their use of sugar.[29]

Significantly, Robert May includes preserves and conserves with distillation and candying in a section also on foods for dieting and for the sick. In contrast to his contemporaries, he refers to all these receipts as 'secrets'. But since he does so in his address to Master Cooks and Young Practitioners, this word may be present in the sense of professional or trade secrets. This in itself is significant, since cookery practice had not had the sense of 'trade' until this time. Along with this is the sense of schooling for cookery. The support system for training cooks by apprenticeship to the kitchens of the gentry must have greatly been disrupted during the Commonwealth period, and as society changed so did the methods for training. This last aspect becomes very important over the later years of the seventeenth century and is a major factor in the gradual specialisation of sugar-work into the confectionery arts.

During the final stage of books relating to 'banquetting stuffe', one watches the change of role parallel the changing position of the audience for these books. Hannah Woolley's *Queenlike Closet . . . Rich Cabinet of Rare Receipts [for] . . . Ingenious Persons of the Female Sex* (1670) presents two sections only in its early editions: one on sugar-work and one on medicine; later editions add a section on 'advice'. And the work is geared to the emerging group of women who no longer have a supportive community structure and have to earn their living in an increasingly commercial economic structure.

Hannah Woolley was responding to specific changes in class structure and social needs. Greater numbers of women were educated, many more needed to support themselves, and many others needed advice on how to behave in new social situations. The mistress of the household was taking on much greater responsibility with the breakdown of extended families; urban life, disease-ridden and unhealthy, was becoming more common and less escapable. In contrast to *A Queen's Closet* (1655), which opens with a list of aristocratic subscribers,[30] Woolley's *Queenlike Closet* is prefaced with an account of her rise in life from servant to gentlewoman. The book is intended to help others do likewise.

One of the many interesting features of the *Queenlike Closet* is the staunch claim that the section on medicine is specifically for the 'Female Sex': it is straightforward, neither 'confounding' the brain nor using 'vain' expressions. Earlier compilations in this period aimed the medical sections at men. The shift here may have as much to do with the ineffectiveness of doctors in the recent plague year of 1665, which must have brought home the need for domestic medicine, as with the emergence of nursing as a vocational opportunity for women. Doctors were expensive, and apothecaries notorious for their abuse of the trade.[31]

But the most significant aspect of the book, or rather the most significant absence, is that of cookery. Woolley did not dismiss cookery, indeed she wrote entire books of recipes,[32] but clearly for this publication she was aiming at the woman who needed a way of earning a living. This exclusion of cookery but inclusion of sugar-work indicates that, while at this time cookery was not a career for women, sugar-work was not only an 'accomplishment' to the gentlewoman but also a skill and artifice which could turn the 'ingenious person of the female sex' into a self-supporting confectioner.

The practice of these skills as a gentleman's accomplishment gradually fades towards the end of the seventeenth century. One of the last books addressing this audience was the *True Preserver and Restorer of Health . . . by T.D.* T.D. was a follower of Sir Kenelm Digby, whose *Closet* contained many recipes for drinks and some for sweetmeats and cookery. Indeed the *True Preserver* is dedicated to Digby's daughter and uses many of his recipes, simply organising them and extending the cookery section. T.D. claims that in the part on medicine he is making receipts public so that the 'private person or Mistress of a family may prepare their own Physick', indicating again the change in attitude of the post-plague years. The book is one of the last in England for over a century to conflate cookery with explicit concern for the treatment of illness and maintenance of health, and also one of the last to incorporate the scientific into the culinary.

A later work with similar concerns but with no intention of providing receipts, is the splendid Thomas Tryon's *Health's Grand Preservative or the Woman's Best Doctor* (1682), which lashes out against the abuses of drink and tobacco by women and children. In *The Good Housewife made a Doctor* (1692), Tryon inveighs against the high costs of medical care and calls for women to take responsibility for preserving health. The jeopardy to health is primarily seen in terms of sugar and strong liquor, with the remedy being a careful control of diet: the introduction speaks of the 'Baneful Mysteries of

Preserving, Conserving etc.' where sugar destroys rather than preserves fruit. While Tryon states (p.107) that sugar-cane is a good fruit if not taken to excess, he launches into an extraordinary tirade against the course of sweetmeats at the end of a meal, the banquet:

> no sooner have they by Gluttony, or eating of too great quantities of Flesh, fish, or other Rich-foods or over-strong liquors brought themselves out of order, but away they run or send Jillian the Chambermaid (who already spoil'd her Teeth with sweet-meats and Kisses) to the Closet for some Conserves, Preserves, or other Confectionary-Ware; and if that will not do (as alas! how should such sower abortive things, only Embalm'd with nauseous Sugar, do any good?) then fetch the Bottle of Black-Cherry-Brandy, the Glas of Aqua Mirabilis, and after that a dose of Plague-water.

But Tryon was a voice crying in the wilderness. For sugar-work, the way forward was firmly into confectionery. *The True Way of Preserving and Candying ... Sweet Meats* (1695) was produced for a school of confectionery, probably by Mary Tillinghast,[33] where apprentices went through six years of training. Interestingly, this book specifically notes that other writings on the topic are a 'ready way to spoil sugar and fruit, rather than to preserve sweet meats'. Although the book is partly a publicity exercise for the school, it is also one of the forerunners of the specialised confectionery books, produced mainly for career women who may have supplied the sweetmeats for the remnants of the banquet that linger on in the early eighteenth-century ambogue. The introduction to *Mrs Mary Eales's Receipts* (1718),[34] a book devoted to sugar-cookery, indicates that Mary Eales may, indeed, have been one such supplier of confectionery to the Court, and that there was at this time a distinct department for confectionery within the Royal Household. As for the ambogue, it is another topic, but it is interesting to note that 1688 reference to the word 'ambigu' in the *London*

Gazette.[35] This composite repast included some of the fare of the sweetmeat banquet, but combined it with other dishes more appropriate to a supper, as William King makes clear:

> When straiten'd in your time and servants few
> You'll rightly them compose an *Ambigue*
> Where first and second course and your Desert
> All in a single Table have their part.[36]

Sweetmeats made by most other women were not, it seems, for banquets; and they rarely claimed any medicinal value. The large compilations, dictionaries, and encyclopedias which arose during the early eighteenth century had separate sections on cookery, confectionery, and domestic medicine, but they were included as part of a very different kind of organisation and along with many different topics. What is quite clear is that, at the level in which they are included in these works, neither sugar-work nor domestic medicine is considered as secret. Eliza Smith in *The Compleat Housewife or Accomplish'd Gentlewoman's Companion* (1727) links the seventeenth-century gentlewoman and the new breed of eighteenth-century urban housewife together in her book's claim both to maintain the 'family' and provide guidance for 'publick-spirited women'. By the end of the seventeenth century not only 'banquetting stuffe' but also the books which conveyed receipts about it had accommodated both to a wider audience and a different class, and to the predominant urban division of women's lives into the commercial and the domestic.

Notes

1. See C. A. Wilson, *The Book of Marmalade* (London, 1985), for an outline of these three main areas of sugar use.
2. See the accompanying essays in this book for a background to the social practices associated with the banquet.
3. I have often wondered if medicinal fashion was at the root of the long-running debate about whether to serve cheese or dessert last in the meal.
4. *The Oxford English Dictionary* (1970), cities two references for

the emergence of the word during the 1530s: 1534, Berners; and 1533, Coverdale.

5. Claude Valgelas, *Conservation de Santé,* translated by H. de Monteux (Paris, 1572).

6. *The Oxford English Dictionary,* as above, gives an occurrence of 'soteltie' from 1517.

7. E. Welsford, *The Court Masque* (Cambridge, 1927); see also the earlier reference to a feast's 'solace' in the *Alliterative Morte Arthure, c.* 1400, II. pp.174–201, pointed out to me by Lesley Johnson.

8. *Handbook of Dates for Students of English History.*

9. See the holdings of the British Library in *The British Museum Catalogue* (London, 1959–75), for an indication of the numbers of the editions.

10. Quoted from T. Elyot, *The Bankette of Sapience* (London, 1539), by S. Lohmberg in *Sir Thomas Elyot, Tudor Humanist* (Austin, 1960) p.130.

11. L. Leys, *The Temperate Man,* 1613, translated by J. Starkey. New ed. (London, 1678).

12. Anne Wilson of the Brotherton Library kindly directed me to 'A Medieval Book of Herbs and Medicine', by E. Brunskill, in *Northwestern Naturalist* n.s., I (1953-4), for this information.

13. This progression of science into private experiment from F. Bacon's insistence on experimental observation as the heart of the scientific method.

14. U. Schumacher-Voelker discusses this phenomenon in 'German Cookery Books 1485–1800', *Petits Propos Culinaires* 6 (1980), p.40.

15. Hugh Platt was an extraordinary early technologist who, for example in *The Jewel House of Art and Nature* (London, *c.* 1594), proposes dried parsnips as a source for sugar. The related sugar-beet did not go into production in England until the early nineteenth century.

16. W. Harrison in Holinshed's Chronicles, 1586, quoted in 'The Ladies of Elizabeth's Court', in *Early English Meals and Manners,* ed. F. J. Furnivall (Early English Text Society, OS32, 1868), p.xc.

17. A mention of the colour yellow for ruffs is made by Dodsley in connection with the Overbury plot, suggesting that the colour yellow was associated with the bands of a Mrs Turner, who went to the scaffold in 1615. *Albumazar* by T. Tomkins, ed. W. Hazlitt, *A Select Collection of Old English Plays, II* (London, 1875), p.328. I am grateful to Dr Martin Butler for pointing this out to me.

18. Prospect Books has printed a facsimile of the 1654 edition (London, 1985), and M. Bell in the introduction outlines a history of the book.

19. *Encyclopaedia Britannica* (1974), I, p.453.

20. The Commonwealth period is generally credited with having

lessened the powers of many of the guilds, the printers being a significant exception to the rule.

21. G. M. Trevelyan, *English Social History* (London, 1944), p.246.
22. M. Plant, *The English Book Trade* (London: George Allen and Unwin, 1974), p.86.
23. See, for example, S. Rowbotham, *Women, Resistance and Revolution* (London, 1972).
24. J. Cromwell, *The Court and Kitchin of Elizabeth* (London, 1664), p.44.
25. For this attribution see E. David 'A True Gentlewoman's Delight', *Petit Propos Culinaires* (1979), p.43.
26. J. Ferguson, *Bibliographical Notes on Histories of Inventions and Books of Secrets*, II (London, 1981), sixth suppl., p.47.
27. Wilson, *The Book of Marmalade*.
28. L. Lemery, *A Treatise on Foods in General* (London, 1704).
29. Interestingly the word 'banket' is still in use in the Dutch language, to refer to sweet, spiced-baked goods.
30. This list goes through an interesting social shift. The edition of 1674 presents the order beginning with King/Queen, Doctor, Guild Master, Lord, Lady, etc., and ending with Mistress and then Master. The 1710 edition completely omits Guild Master and begins with Queen and Bishop, ending with Doctor, Mister, and Mistress.
31. See T. Cocke, *Kitchin-Physicke* (London, 1676).
32. See U. Schumacher-Volker, 'The Authorship of *The Accomplish'd Lady's Delight*, 1675'. *Petits Propos Culinaires* (1981), p.66, for a discussion of the attribution of the *Accomplisht Ladies Delight* (1675).
33. M. Tillinghast had already published an earlier book on pastry-cooking, *Rare and Excellent Receipts* (London, 1690 2nd edn).
34. M. Eales, *Mrs. Mary Eales's Receipts* (London, 1985 , reprinted from 1733 edn).
35. *The Oxford English Dictionary*.
36. W. King, *The Art of Cookery* (London, 1709), p.97. For an idea of the contents of an 'ambigu', see the menu outlines in C. Carter, *The Compleat Practical Cook* (London, 1985, reprinted from 1733 edn).

4.

Rare Conceites and Strange Delightes: The Practical Aspects of Culinary Sculpture

PETER BREARS

'Banquet The banquet course provided a unique opportunity for
stuffe' the display of culinary skills, artistic flair, theatrical effect,
and sheer wealth. The combination of elaborate
sculptural creations in sugar, with sweetmeats, fruit and
nuts all highly finished either in naturalistic colours or
gilded with gold leaf were the most magnificent
assemblies of dishes ever to have been presented on
English tables.

Some indication of their range and variety is given in
the following account from Randle Holme's *The Academy
of Armoury* of 1688:[1]

1. March-pan set with several sorts of Sweet-Meats.
2. Preserves or wet Sweet-Meats in Plates as, Pears,
Plums, Cherries, Quinces, Grapes, Respass, Pippins,
Oranges, Lemmons, young Walnuts, Apricocks,
Peaches, &c with their Syrup about them.
3. Dried Sweet-meats and suckets of Oranges,
Lemmons, Citron: or Conserves, or Candies, and
Rock-Candies of Cherries, Apricocks, Plums,
Damasins, Pippins, Pears, Angelica, Rosemary and
Marygold Flowers, Pippins, Pears, Apricocks, Plums,
Ringo roots: or Marmalet of Quinces, Damasins,
Plums, Oranges, etc. Pastes made of Citron: Pippins,
Apricocks, Rasbery, English Currans.
4. Biskets, Mackroons, naple Bisket, Italian Bisket,

Comfeits round, Longe and Loseng like, Gingerbread, Almond Cakes, Apricock Cakes, Losenges, Quince Chips, Orange cakes, Marchpane Collops.

5. Sugar cakes, Jamballs, Jemelloes, Sugar Plate, Plum and Rasbury cakes, Cheesecakes.

6. Tree Fruit as Apples and Pears of diverse kinds, Cherries, Plums, Strawberries, Currans, Raspes, Walnut, Chestnuts, Filbernuts, Dates, Graps, Figgs, Oranges, Lemmons, Apricocks, Peech, Dried Raisins and Currans, Prunes, Almonds blanched.

According to the season for them, all which several things are mixt and inter-changably set on the Table according to the description of the Gentleman Sewer.

There were also jellies of five or six colours, creams made of codlings, quince, plums, goosberries or almonds, clouted cream, snow cream, fresh cheese and cream, syllabubs, egg pies, custards, white pots, fools, leach, blamangers, lay tarts of diverse colours, tarts royal, codlings and cream cheese.

In the following pages a range of these dishes is discussed in further detail, with both contemporary descriptions and recipes given in modern form to enable them to be re-created for use today.

Marchpanes

The marchpane, the centrepiece of any banquet, was a large disc of almond paste, iced, decorated, and surmounted, for special occasions, with three-dimensional figures or models in cast sugar, sugar-plate, or almond paste. In 1562 Queen Elizabeth's 'Surveiour of the Workes' gave her a marchpane bearing a model of St Paul's Cathedral; while from Robert Hickes, Yeoman of the Chamber, came a 'very faire marshpane made like a tower, with men and artillery in it', and from her Master Cook, George Webster, a 'faire marchpane being a chessboarde'. They were quite expensive, Lord North buying ten for £5 when entertaining Queen Elizabeth in 1577.[2]

5.
Marchpane stuffe, a stiff paste of ground almonds and sugar, could be used to produce a variety of delicacies, including 'collops of bacon' (1); while sugar-plate, made of icing sugar strengthened with gum, was used for artificial walnuts (2), cinnamon sticks (3), cards (4), and the muscadines commonly called 'kissing comfits' (5).

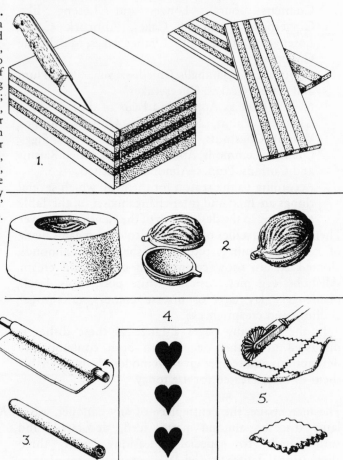

To make a Marchpane

Take halfe a pound of blanched Almonds, and of white Suger a quarter of a pound, of Rose-water halfe an ounce, & of Damaske water as much: beat the Almonds with a little of the same water, and grind them till they be small; set them on a few coales of fire till they waxe thick, then beate them againe with suger, fine: then mixe the sweet waters and them together, and so gather them, and fashion your Marchpane: then take wafer cakes of the broadest making, cut them square, past them together with a little liquor, and when you have made them as broad as will serve your purpose, have ready a hoop of a greene hazel wand, of ye thicknesse of halfe an inch, on the inner side smooth, without any knags: lay this hoope upon your Wafer cakes aforesaid and then fill your hoope with the geare above named, ye same driven smooth above with the back of a silver spoone, as ye doo a Tarte, and cut away all parts of the cakes, even close by the outside of the hoop, with a sharpe knife, that it may be round: then having white paper underneath it, set it upon a warme hearth, or upon an instrument of yron or brasse, made for the same purpose, or into an Oven, after the bread is taken out, so it be not stopped: it may not bake, but only be hard and thorow dryed, and ye may while it is moyst stick it full of Comfets of sundry colours, in a comely order, yee must moist it over with Rose-water and suger together: make it smooth, and set it into the oven or other instrument, the cleerer it is like a Lanterne horne, so much the more commended. If it be through dried, and kept in a dry and warme ayr, a Marchpane will last many yeeres. It is a comfortable meate meet for weake folks, such as have lost the taste of meates by much and long sicknes. The greatest secret that is in making thys cleere, it with a little fine flower of Rice, Rosewater and suger beaten together, and layd thin over the Marchpane ere it goe to drying. This will make it shine, like Ice, as Ladies report.

[*The Treasurie of Hidden Secrets*, 1600]

To make the basic marchpane paste take:

1 lb (450 g) ground almonds

8 oz (250 g) caster sugar
1–2 tbls (15–30 ml) rosewater

and work it to a stiff paste in a mortar and pestle or food processor, or work 4 oz (100 g) ground almonds into 1 lb (450 g) ready-made white almond paste to produce a stiff paste.

Originally the paste was then rolled out onto a layer of wafers, but today a piece of greaseproof paper will fulfil the same purpose. Roll the paste into a circle, about $\frac{3}{8}$ inches in thickness, then turn up the edge and impress with a fork or the back of a knife, just like the edge of a pie. In the traditional beehive ovens the marchpane could be baked at a gentle heat for long periods in a hot, dry atmosphere. With today's ovens this can be imitated by baking it at 300°F, gas mark 3, for 15 minutes and then allowing it to cool slowly for a further 15 minutes with the oven door open, this process being repeated until the marchpane is firm and dry but only lightly coloured. To glaze the marchpane, then take:

1 tbls (15 ml) rosewater
3 tbls (45ml) icing sugar

mix them to a thin paste, brush over the marchpane, and bake at 300°F, gas mark 3, for 5–10 minutes, examining it from time to time, and taking it from the oven when dry and glossy, but not white and frothed.

Having cooled, the marchpane can be decorated by having any of the following stuck into its surface to form patterns or pictures:

(a) caraway comfits stuck up on end. If these are not available, small coloured sweets make a good substitute, as do confectioners' silver balls;

(b) lozenges, pieces of sugar-plate cut into small diamond-shapes using zig-zag pastry jigger, see sugar-plate below;

(c) jumbals or knot biscuits, see below;

(d) 'standards', three-dimensional ornaments or figures, see cast-sugar below;

(e) modelled features made from marchpane paste;

(f) gilded pictures, decorations or inscriptions.

The technique for gilding is given in some detail in *The Treasurie of Hidden Secrets* of 1600:

> To gild a Marchpane or any other kind of Tart. Take and cut your leafe of gold, as it lieth upon the booke into square pieces like dice, & with a Conies tayles end moisted a little, take the gold by the one corner, lay it on the place, being first made moist, and with another tayle of a Conie dry, presse the gold down close, And if you will have the forme of an Hart, or the name of Jesus or any other strange thing whatsoever, cut the same through a peece of paper and lay the paper upon your Marchpane or Tarte: then make the voyde place of the paper moyst with Rosewater, lay on your golde, presse it down, take off your paper, and there remaineth behind in gold, the print cut in the same paper.

The almond paste used for making marchpanes can also be used for other purposes, *A Closet for Ladies and Gentlewomen* of 1611 recommends modelling 'conceits of March-pane stuffe, some like pyes, birds, baskets, and such like & some print with moulds [see cast-sugar, below]. They be excellent good to please children.' It can also be made as follows:

'Marchpane stuffe'

> To make calishones
>
> Take halfe a pound of Marchpane paste, a thimble-full of coriander seeds beaten to a powder, with a graine of Muske, beat all to a perfect paste, print it and drie it. [John Murrell *A Daily Exercise and Ladies and Gentlewomen,* 1617, p.85.]

Mix one teaspoon (5 ml) of ground coriander into 8 oz (225 g) almond paste, print it, and dry it.

> To make collops like Bacon of Marchpane
>
> Take some of your Marchpane Paste, and work it in red Saunders till it be red; then rowl a broad sheet of

white paste, and a sheet of red Paste, three of the white, and four of the red, and so one upon another in mingled sorts, every red between, then cut it overthwart, till it look like Collops of Bacon, then dry it. [W. M., *A Queens Delight*, 1671 edn, p.69.]

Divide 12 oz (325 g) of the paste in two, and knead a few drops of food colouring into one half to give it a lean bacon colour. Using either cornflour or icing sugar to dust the paste, roll out half the white mixture into a rectangle about $^3/_8$ inches (10 mm) in thickness, and the remainder into three thinner rectangles of the same size. Divide the red paste into four, and roll out each piece to the same size. Starting with the thick slab of 'fat' build up alternate red and white layers to form a miniature piece of streaky bacon, from which thin collops or slices are cut and allowed to dry in a warm place.

Decorations

The almond paste can be used for direct modelling, to produce 'letters, knots, Armes, Escocheons, birds and other fancies' (Sir Hugh Platt, *Delightes for Ladies*, 1609, p.18).

To make white gingerbread

Take halfe a pound of marchpaine past, a quarter of a pound of white ginger beaten and cerst, halfe a pound of the powder of refined sugar, beat this to a very fine paste with dragagant [gum tragacanth] steept in rose-water, then roule it in round cakes and print it with your moulds: dry them in an oven when the breade is drawne foorth; upon white papers, & when they be very dry, box them, and keepe them all the yeare. [John Murrell, *A Delightful Daily Exercise for Ladies and Gentlewomen*, 1621]

8 oz (225 g) almond paste
4 tsp (20 ml) ground ginger
8 oz (225 g) icing sugar
2 tbls (30 ml) rosewater
1 tsp (5 ml) gelatine

Mix the gelatine with the rosewater in a cup, and place in a pan of hot water to melt. Mix the ginger and sugar in a bowl, pour in the melted gelatine and rosewater, and work together to form a stiff paste. Add the almond paste, which has been kneaded to a plastic state, and knead the two pastes together to form a uniform light brown mixture. This can then be rolled into a thin sheet, printed or cut out, and allowed to dry.

Cast-sugar work was perhaps the most impressive, and the **Cast-sugar** most difficult, of all the highly decorated dishes which appeared at the banquet table. It was used to make all kinds of birds, beasts, fruits, and the other three-dimensional figures or 'standards' necessary for decorating marchpanes, etc., in which the cook could fully demonstrate his skill in technique and design. In 1600 Sir Hugh Platt gave full instructions on how:

> To make both marchpane paste, and sugred plate,
> And cast the same in formes of sweetest grace
> Each bird and foule, so moulded from the life,
> And after cast in sweet compounds of Arte,
> As if the flesh and forme which Nature gave,
> Did still remaine in every lim and part.

Work of this kind began with the preparation of a number of moulds. These might be made in stone, wood, or pewter by a craftsman with the required skills, but probably most moulds were made of 'alabaster', or plaster of Paris, by the cooks themselves. Taking actual objects, such as a pheasant with its plumage smeared down to a smooth surface, or an orange or a lemon, plaster was poured over first one section and then another to produce a mould which could be dismantled to remove its contents. The dry plaster was then soaked in cold water for a period varying from an hour to overnight, depending on the recipe. Having been dried with a cloth, it was assembled, its sections tied securely together with tape, and a syrup of sugar boiled to a hard crack (325°F) poured in. The mould was then rotated in the hand to spread an even layer of sugar around the interior, allowed to cool, and then opened to reveal a complete sugar creature or fruit. This could finally be decorated either in its natural colours or with gold-leaf gilding.[3] For details of boiling the sugar to the correct state, see *The Constance Spry Recipe Book* (1967 edn.) pp.858–61.

Sugar-plate   Sugar-plate is a remarkably versatile modelling medium, capable of being made into all manner of sweets, models, or even plates and glasses which can be put to practical use:

> To make a paste of Suger, whereof a man may make all manner of fruits, and other fine things with their forme, as Plates, Dishes, Cuppes, and such like thinges, wherewith you may furnish a Table: Take Gumme and dragant [gum tragacanth] as much as you wil, and steep it in Rosewater till it be mollified, and for four ounces of suger take of it the bignes of a beane, the juyce of Lemons, a Walnut shel ful, and a little of the white of an eg. But you must first take the gumme, and beat it so much with a pestell in a brazen morter, till it be come like water, then put it to the juyce with the white of an egge, incorporating al thes wel together, this don take four ounces of fine white suger well beaten to powder, and cast it into ye morter by a little and little until they be turned into ye form of paste, then take it out of the said morter, and bray it upon the powder of suger, as it were meale or flower, untill it be like soft paste, to the end you may turn it, and fashion it which way you wil. When you have brought your paste to this fourme spread it abroad upon great or smal leaves as you shall think it good, and so shal you form or make what things you wil, as aforesaid, with such fine knackes as may serve a Table taking heede there stand no hotte thing nigh it. At the end of the Banket they may eat all, and breake

the Platters, Dishes, Glasses, Cuppes, and all other things, for this paste is very delicate and saverous. [*The Second Part of the Good Hus-wives Jewell*, 1597, p.39] To make the paste, take:

> ½ tsp (2.5 ml) gelatine
> 1 tsp (5 ml) lemon juice
> 2 tsps (10 ml) rosewater
> ½ egg white, lightly beaten
> 12–16 oz (250–450 g) icing sugar
> A few drops of food colouring, if required

Stir the gelatine into the lemon juice and rosewater in a basin and place over a bowl of hot water until melted. Stir in the egg white, add food colouring and work in the icing sugar, little by little, until a dough is formed. It can then be turned out on a board dusted with icing sugar, kneaded until completely smooth, rolled out, and used as required to make:

Fruit trenchers

These were discs of sugar-plate some 5 inches in diameter and under an ⅛ of an inch in thickness, which served as plates during the banquet course. Having dried to complete hardness, they were hand painted with elaborate designs, using a variety of colourings bound with rosewater and gum, ground cinnamon being used for dark brown, cinnamon and ginger for light brown, saffron for yellow, 'Roset' [unidentified red dye] for 'murrie' [mulberry colour] and sap green for green.[4] Fortunately, a number of sycamore fruit trenchers of the same size, shape, and purpose as the sugar-plate trenchers still survive in museum collections, thus enabling the decorative treatment of banqueting trenchers to be reproduced exactly (see illus. 13). Finally, the edges of the trenchers were gilded 'with the white of an egge laide rounde about the brim of the dish with a pensill [i.e. a fine paint brush], and presse the gold down with some cotton, & when it is drie skew or brush off the golde with the foot of a hare or Conie'.[5]

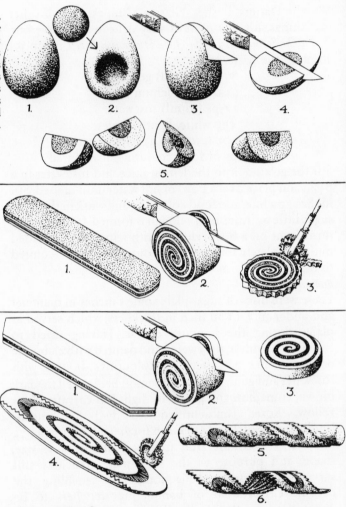

6.
Margaret Savile's Recipe Book of 1683 gives detailed instructions for modelling eggs (top), round cakes (middle) and ribbons (bottom) in mixtures of white and coloured sugar-plate.

Plates and wine glasses

These were made of sugar-plate and were used just like pottery and glass vessels on the banqueting table, being quite waterproof for an hour or two, although they were unable to withstand heat. Having rolled out the prepared paste, dusting it with cornflour, it is pressed into saucers, plates, or the bowls of wine glasses to mould it into the required shapes. The surplus trimmed from the rims may then be modelled in the form of baluster stems and bases, either for the glasses or to convert the saucers into standing tazzas for the better display of sweetmeats etc. Once the various sections have stiffened, they may be turned out of their supporting saucers, wine glasses, etc., and allowed to harden completely before being stuck together as required with a little icing. They will then resemble vessels of the finest porcelain, being pure white, translucent, and thin and strong if well made. Even so, they may be snapped into pieces and eaten at the end of the banquet.

Moulded decorations

Sugar-plate paste kneaded with additional icing sugar to make it quite stiff, makes an excellent moulding material. It may be dusted with cornflower to prevent it sticking, and then pressed into specially carved wooden moulds, the surplus being trimmed off with a knife before inverting the mould and knocking one end against the table top to free the sugar-plate impression. Using detailed moulds, thin slabs of sugar plate can thus be formed into the walls of boxes or miniature houses, their edges being mitred and stuck together with royal icing to produce strong three-dimensional structures. Alternatively, moulds can be made from plaster of Paris, as in the following:

> To make walnuts artificial
>
> Take searsed Sugar, and Cinnamon, of quantity alike work it up with a little Gum Dragon, steep it in Rose-water, and print it in a mould made like a Walnut-shell, then take white Sugar Plates, print it in a mould made like a Walnut kernel, so when they are both dry, close them up together with a little Gum Dragon betwixt, and they will dry as they lie. [W.M., *A Queens Delight*, 1671 edn, p.69; see also *A Closet for Ladies and Gentlewomen . . .* 1611, p.33]

Take a wooden walnut mould, or make a plaster mould by cracking a walnut carefully in two, smearing the halves with a thick grease, such as petroleum jelly, and placing them in the bottom of a disposable plastic container. Cover with plaster of Paris, allow it to set, then remove from the container and carefully take out the walnut shells. The mould should be dried out for a few days in a warm place before being used. Knead ground cinnamon into the sugar-paste until it is the colour of a walnut shell, then break pieces off, dust them with further cinnamon, and press into the moulds in a layer one-eighth of an inch or less in thickness. Trim off the surplus, remove from the mould, and allow to dry. The halves can then be filled with kernels similarly cast in white sugar-plate, with caraway comfits or small sweets, with a verse of poesie written on a small scroll, or with a stiff fruit cheese, such as quince marmalade, and then stuck together with a little icing.

Cinnamon Sticks

Take of Cinamon & Ginger, of each a like quantity being finely searsed, mingle it with your searsed sugar, and Gum-tragacant steeped in Rose-water, and worke it into Past,...you may then turn it upon sticks made of peeces of arrowes, and make them hollow like Cinamon stickes ... [*A Closet for Ladies and Gentlewomen*, 1611, p.26]

Knead ground cinnamon and ginger in equal quantities into the sugar-plate until it is the colour of cinnamon, then roll it out as thinly as possible, dusting with further cinnamon to prevent sticking, and 'turn it upon sticks made of peeces of arrowes, and make them hollow like Cinamon stickes';

Cards

And if you would have paste exceeding smooth, as to make cardes and such like conceipts thereof, then roule your paste upon a sliked paper with a smooth and polished rolling pin. [Sir Hugh Platt, *Delightes for Ladies*, 1609, p.13]

Roll out the sugar-plate as thinly as possible on a smooth surface, dusting it with cornflour to prevent sticking. Cut into the shape of playing cards and, when dry, paint it with hearts, clubs, spades, and diamonds to resemble playing cards.

To Make Muscadines, commonly called Kissing Comfits

then slicke a sheet of white paper, slicked with a slick-stone very smooth, and rowle your sugar paste upon it, then cut it like lozenges with a rowel, & so dry them upon a stone, and when they bee dry they will serve to garnish a marchpaine, or other dishes, tarts, custards, or whatsoever else, if you will have any red you must mingle Rosa Paris, if blew with blew bottles growing in the corn [cornflowers]. [John Murrell, *A Delightfull Daily Exercise for Ladies and Gentlewomen,* 1621]

Cut the rolled-out white, red, or blue sugar-paste into small diamonds, using a pastry jigger, allow to dry, and use them as sweets, or to decorate marchpanes, tarts, custards, etc.

Bacon

Follow the instructions given for marchpane bacon (see p. 000).

Eggs

Take a piece of the white Paste, & roll itt in your hand like an Egge, then make a hole in the middle of itt and putt a piece of your yellow-Paste [in] & so close it well together in your hand, then cut itt in two, & cut each halfe in pieces like the quarters of an egge. [*Margaret Saville's MS Recipe Book,* 1683, Yorkshire Archaeological Society, DD148.]

Make an egg shape in white sugar-plate. Make a hollow in the side, insert a yellow sugar-plate 'yolk', and seal over with the white. Cut the egg in quarters and allow to dry.

Round Cakes

Take a little piece of your white Paste, & roule itt with

a rouling-pinne in a narrow long piece, then lay a piece of coloured Paste upon itt, & then lay a piece of white againe upon itt, & what other colour you please (having them all before you) upon itt also, then close them well together with your hand, & so rowle up your Paste, & cut them into little cakes, & run your Jagging-Iron about them. [*Margaret Savile's Recipe Book*, 1683]

Roll out identical thin strips of sugar-plate, two being white, and two of different colours. Lay them on top of each other, alternating the white and the colours, roll them up to form a cylinder, and cut it across with a sharp knife to make discs showing a spiral pattern. Roll out each disc into a thin round, and cut into a neat circle with a pastry jigger.

Ribbons

To make your Ribbin roule two long narrow pieces of white & lay a piece of your coloured Paste, then lay your piece of coloured Paste between your two pieces of white Paste, & thrust itt downe with your finger, then fasten itt downe with your rowling- pinne, cut both ends sharpe like an arrow-head, then roll itt upp like a collar of Brawne, then close itt close in the clutches of your hand, then cutt of pieces of the ends, then roule them out at length, then cutt off the sides of it with your Jagging-Irons, then wrap itt about a small stick, & so let itt stand a little till itt is dry, and then you may slip forth the stick ... For your sticks you rolled your Ribbin on let them not bee longer then your hand, which is long enough for any fruit-dish, they need bee noe thicker than your finger. If you will have shadowed Ribbin, in the same manner as you did this between two whites, put several colours. [*Margaret Savile's Recipe Book*, 1683]

Roll out two long strips of white sugar-plate and one of coloured sugar-plate. Sandwich the colour between the white, and roll up into a cylindrical form. Cut the cylinder into broad slices and roll out each slice into a long strip. Trim the edges with a pastry jigger to form a long ribbon, which is finally wound around a small stick to form a spiral ribbon.

Creams and butters formed an important part of the banquet, being either spooned from their dishes, scooped up with wafers, or eaten with brown bread, as Samuel Pepys recorded in his diary for 13 July 1665.

Creams and butters

In their simplest form, creams were made by whipping double cream with a whisk made of hard white rushes until it was very thick, but not turned to butter, this being laid in the dish with a spatula, and sprinkled with sugar. Alternatively the cream could be clotted, as described by Sir Kenelm Digby:[6]

> Take two Gallons more or less of new milk, set it upon a clear fire; when it is ready to boil, put in a quart of sweet cream, and take it off the fire, and strain through a hire sieve into earthen pans; let it stand two days and two nights; then take it off with a skimmer; strew sugar on the cream, and serve it to the Table.

or it could be thickened by boiling, as in the following recipes:

To make a Sack Cream

Set a quart of cream on the fire, when it is boyled, drop in a spoonful of Sack and stir it well the while that it curd not, so do till you have dropped in six spoonfuls, then season it with Sugar, Nutmeg and strong water. [W.M., *The Compleat Cook*, 1655, p.33]

> 1 pt (575 ml) single cream
> 3 tbs (45 ml) dry sherry
> 1 tbs (15 ml) caster sugar
> pinch of ground nutmeg

Boil the cream, gradually stir in the sherry, then the sugar and nutmeg, and chill before serving.

Lemon-cream

Boyle in some Creame the Pill of a Lemon, a lumpe of Sugar, & when itt is boyle and pretty cool, put to itt the juice of Lemon & as much sugar as you think fitt, and sprinkle some long thin slices of Lemon-Pill on the top of itt after itt is dished. [*Margaret Savile's Receipe Book*, 1683]

7.
Creams and jellies for the banquet, including: 'Spannish papps' (1), ice cream (2), syllabub (3), jelly lemons (4), leach (5) and 'ye jelly . . . in careless lumps' (6).

1 pt (575 ml) single cream
1 tbs (15 ml) caster sugar
1 lemon

Pare the zest from the lemon, and boil it with the cream
and sugar. When cool remove the zest, place cream in
serving dish, and gradually stir in the juice of the lemon,
then decorate with the zest cut in fine straws.

Ice-cream

Ice-houses, in which the ice of winter could be preserved
throughout the year, first appeared in the royal palaces in
the 1660s, thus permitting ice-cooled fruit drinks,
sherbets, wines, and frozen creams to be served at great
official celebrations and feasts. By the mid-eighteenth
century, many large country houses boasted similar
facilities, and ice-cream enjoyed a much wider usage
among the upper classes. The recipe book of Grace,
Countess Granville gives the following late seventeenth-
century instructions:

The Ice Creame

Take a fine pan Like a pudding pan $\frac{1}{2}$ a $\frac{1}{4}$ of a yard
deep, and the bredth of a Trencher; take your Cream
and sweeton it with Sugar and 3 Spoonfulls of
Orrange flower water, & fill yor. pan full, yn. cover itt
wth. a Tin cover, & lay it close up wth. Batter; have
redy a coarse cloath Laid on ye. ground and break yor.
Ice in pretty Lumps have reddy 3d of Salt pettor, 2d of
Roch allum 3d of bay Salt, beat ye Allum and Salt
peetor very well & mingle it wth. yr. Ice and bay Salt.
Lay Some [of] this into a Stean pott, yn. set yor.
Creame on ye Ice on yr. pott and strow ye rest all over
it, and yn. clap ye Cloath all over ye pott and wch.
will be immediately frose; yn. Let it stand just 2 hours
and no Longer; order yor. time to yor. dinner exactly;
take yor. warm hand and work about ye pan to
Loosen ye Creame yn. it may turn out on a Salver,
first take of all ye Buttor send quick to yr. Table or it

will melt againe. [see Elizabeth David, in *Petit Propos Culinaires*, 2, 1979, p.27]

2 pt (1150 ml) double cream
4 tbs (60 ml) caster sugar
3 tbs (45 ml) orangeflower water
1 watertight metal or plastic
straight-sided dish, 4.5 ins (11 cm) high
by 9 ins (23 cm) diameter

Stir the ingredients together until the sugar is dissolved, pour into the dish, cover with a lid or plastic film, and place in a freezer for at least two hours. When required, quickly dip the dish into luke-warm water (this is less painful than using one's hands, as specified in the recipe) to loosen the ice cream, and turn out on to a shallow serving dish.

Thickened creams

As described in the following recipes, the creams could also be thickened with gelatine, rice, rennet, eggs, or alcoholic liquors.

To make Piramidis Cream

Take a quart of water, and six ounces of Harts-Horn, and put it into a Bottle with Gum-dragon, and Gum-arabick, of each as much as a small Nut, put all this into the bottle, which must be so big as will hold a pint more; for if it be full it will break; stop it very close with a cork, and tye a cloath about it, put the bottle into a pot of Beef when it is boyling, and let it boyl three hours, then take as much Cream as there is jelly, and half a pound of Almonds well beaten with Rose-water, so that you cannot discern what they be, mingle the Cream and the Almonds together, then strain it, and do so two or three times to get all you can out of the Almonds, then put Jelly, when it is cold, into a silver Bason, & the Cream to it; sweeten it as you like, put in two or three grains of Musk and Amber-greece, set it over the fire, stirring it continually and skimming it, till it be seething hot, but let it not boyl, then put it into an old-fashioned drinking Glasse, and let it stand till it is cold, and when you will use it, hold your Glasse in a warm hand, and loosen it with a Knife, and whelm it into a dish, and have in readiness Pine-Apple blown [pine nuts] and stick it all over, and serve it with cream or without as you please. [W.M., *The Compleat Cook*, 1655, p.32]

> 2 tbs (30 ml) gelatine
> ½ pt (275 ml) cream
> 1 tbs (15 ml) rosewater
> 2 tbs (30 ml) sugar
> 10 drops almond essence

Dissolve the gelatine and sugar in ½ pt (275 ml) boiling water, and allow to cool, but not set. Stir this, with the remaining ingredients, into the cream, and mould in wetted wine glasses, then turning them out on to plates when set, serve with single cream.

Spannish Papps

R. Rice and wash itt in three several waters, & dry itt three days, then beat itt and searce itt through Lawne, then R. a pint of sweet creame & boyle itt, then let itt coole, then take three whites of eggs well beaten & three spoonfull of the rice-powder and three spoonfull of fine sugar, a little Rose-water, & put all these to the creame, & boil all these till itt is as thick as hastie Pudding, then have six wine glasses wett with Rose-water to put itt in, & when it is cold, turne itt out upon Pye-plates, and garnish itt with sweatmeats and wafers. [*Margaret Savile's Recipe Book*, 1683]

> 1 pt (575 ml) cream
> 2½ oz (65 g) rice flour
> 2½ oz (65 g) sugar
> 2 tsp (10 ml) rosewater
> whites of three eggs

Lightly beat the eggs and mix with the remainder of the ingredients and heat slowly, stirring continuously until the mixture has thickened. Moisten the interior of a number of wine glasses with rosewater, fill with the mixture, and allow to set. Turn the paps out onto plates and garnish with wafers preserved and crystallised fruits, etc.

To make a Summer-dishe, or Trifle

R. a quart of new sweet creame, or of new milke, & putt into itt as much white sugar beaten small as will make itt very sweet, & nutmegge cut into quarters, some whole large mace, 3 good spoonfull of Orange-flower-water, or else as much Rose-water with some Muske or Ambergreece dissolved in it; Let these boyle together a pretty space, then pouring all into a clean and handsome dishe, take out the nutmegge and mace, & presently pour into the dishe three spoonfull of good Rennett, stirring itt gently round about, then let the dish stand covered without jogging till itt bee thoroughly cold, then scatter in some round Comfitts, or for want of Comfits scrape in some hard sugar upon itt, & eat itt as soon as itt is cold; this is an excellent Dishe in summer, a fine meat, being both cooling & pleasing, for it will eat as cool as Ice, & itt will be as a custard to the very bottome. [*Margaret Savile's Recipe Book,* 1683]

1 pt (575 ml) cream
3 tbs (45 ml) sugar
½ whole nutmeg in pieces
2 tsps (10 ml) rosewater or orangeflower water
a few blades of mace
2 tsp (10 ml) rennet

Simmer all the ingredients (except the rennet) together for a few minutes, pour into a dish, allow to cool to blood heat, stir in the rennet, and allow to stand until quite cold. Sprinkle scraped sugar-candy (or sugar) over the top before serving. This summer dish is highly commended: see the final sentence of the original recipe.

To Make a Cream in the Italian Fashion
to eat Cold

Take twenty yolks of eggs, and two quarts of cream,
strain it with a little salt, saffron, rosewater, juyce of
orange, a little white wine and a pound of sugar; then
bake it in a deep dish with some fine cinamon, and
some candied pistaches stuck on it, and when it is
baked, white muscadines. [Robert May, *The
Accomplisht Cook*, 3rd edn. 1671, p.286]

5 egg yolks
1 pt (575 ml) single cream
2 oz (50 g) sugar
1 tbs (15 ml) orange juice
1 tbs (15 ml) sweet white wine
2 tsp (10 ml) rosewater
pinch of safron and of cinnamon
1 tsp (5 ml) sugared pistachio nuts for decoration

Mix together all the ingredients except the nuts, and place
in an ovenproof two-pint dish, standing this in a bowl of
hot water and baking at gas mark 4, 350°F (180°C) for
about 50 minutes, until a knife inserted into the centre
comes out clean. When cold, sprinkle the nuts over the
surface.

A Good Dish of Cream

Boil a quart of good Cream with sticks of Cinnamon
and quartered Nutmeg and Sugar to your taste. When
it is boiled enough to have acquired the taste of the
Spice, take the whites of six New laid eggs, and beat
them very well with a little Fresh-cream, then pour
them to your boyling Cream, and let them boil a
walm or two. Then let it run through a boulter, and
put a little Orange flower-water to it, and sliced
bread; and so serve it up cold. [Sir Kenelm Digby, *The
Closet of Sir Kenelm Digby Opened*, 3rd edn, 1677, p.109]

1 pt (575 ml) cream
1 stick cinnamon
½ nutmeg, in pieces

8.
Tarts for the banquet were frequently presented on the table having had their upper crust removed and replaced by separately baked tart-tops divided into ornamental patterns with pastry strips, and panels of coloured preserves and marmalades. These designs for 'cut-laid tarts' come from Robert May's *Accomplisht Cook* of 1660. The bottom row shows designs for cheesecakes from the same source.

2 oz (50 g) sugar
3 egg whites
3 tbs (15 ml) orangeflower water

Boil the spices, sugar and most of the cream for a few minutes until well flavoured. Beat the eggs with the remaining cream, mix them into the hot cream, and boil up twice before draining in a piece of fine cloth. When cold, mix in the orangeflower water and heap on slices of white bread in a shallow dish.

Syllabubs

For syllabub, the cream was blended with wine, sweetened and flavoured to produce a very rich but delicate dish. It was usually served in small two-handled syllabub glasses made with a miniature spout, almost like a tea-pot, so that the clear wine-rich whey could be drunk separately from the creamy curd above.

My Lady Middlesex makes Syllabubs for little Glasses with spouts, thus. Take 3 pints of sweet cream, one of quick white wine (or Rhenish), and a good wine glassful (better the ¼ of a pint) of Sack: mingle with them about three quarters of a pound of fine Sugar in Powder. Beat all these together with a whisk, till all appeareth converted into froth. Then pour it into your little Syllabub-glasses, and let them stand all night. The next day the curd will be thick and firm above, and the drink clear under it. I conceive it may do well to put into each glass (when you pour the liquor into it) a sprig of Rosemary a little bruised, or a little Limon-peel, or some such thing to quicken the taste; or use Amber-sugar, or spirit of Cinnamon, or of Lignum Cassiac; or Nutmegs, or Mace, or Cloves, a very little. [Sir Kenelm Digby, *The Closet of Sir Kenelm Digby Opened,* 3rd edn, 1677, p.108]

> 1 pt (575 ml) double cream
> 7 fl oz (200 ml) Rhenish white wine
> 2 tbs (30 ml) dry sherry
> 4 oz (125 g) caster sugar

sprigs of rosemary or the peeled zest of a lemon

Beat the cream, wines and sugar together to form a thick froth, and spoon this into large wine glasses. Insert either the rosemary or the lemon into each glass and allow to stand in a cool place for at least twelve hours before serving.

In addition to the flavourings described above, creams

were combined with fruit to give a number of pleasantly sharp-flavoured dishes, such as:

To make gooseberry creams

First boil, or you may preserve your gooseberries, then having a clear cream boiled up and seasoned with old cinnamon, nutmeg, mace, sugar, rosewater and eggs, dish it up and when it is cold take up the gooseberries with a pin and stick them on in rounds as thick as they can lie upon the said cream, garnishing your dish with them, and strow them over with the finest sugar and serve them up. [*The Court and Kitchen of Elizabeth commonly called Joan Cromwell*, 1664, p.60]

Make a dish of cream as described under 'A Good Dish of Cream' and cover it with concentric circles of gooseberries which have been simmered to tenderness (about 10 minutes) in a syrup made with 4 oz (125 g) sugar to half a pint (275 ml) of water.

A Pippin-Creame

R. Pippens pared, core them & quarter them, putt them into a silver Tankard with a little fair water, Orange-flower-water, a little Orange-pill, & a little sugar. sett it in Embers, or a hot oven, let itt stand but till they are soft, then pulpe itt through a Hair-sieve, & put to itt 2 or 3 yolkes of Eggs and cream enough but to make itt of a good thicknesse, put a little Orange on the top. [*Margaret Savile's Recipe Book*, 1683]

1 lb (450 g) cooking apples
¼ pt (150 ml) water
2 tbs (30 ml) orangeflower water
a little pared zest of orange peel
2 oz (50 g) sugar
3 egg yolks
¼ pt (150 ml) double cream

Put all the ingredients except the eggs and cream into a covered pan and simmer gently until cooked. Remove from the heat, blend or rub through a sieve, reheat, take from the stove, mix in the eggs lightly beaten into the cream, pour into the serving dish, and allow to cool.

Butters

Other creams, more usually called butters, frequently contained neither butter nor cream, but received their names from their smooth texture and thick creamy consistency:

Orange Butter

R. a quarter of a Pint [150 ml] of cleared juice of Oranges, a quarter of a Pint [150 ml] of white wine, pare the Peel of your Oranges thinne, steep itt in the juice and white-wine halfe an hour, then put in when you have taken out the pill a little [2 tsp or 10 ml] fine Sugar, to take away the sharpnesse. Then beat the yolks of six eggs very well, & putt them into the liquour, and sett them over the fire, & keep itt continually stirring till you find it almost as thick as Butter, [but do not allow it to boil], then throw itt about the dish or bason, and let itt stand all night, in the morning take itt off lightlie with a spoon, & serve itt as other Butter. [*Margaret Savile's Recipe Book,* 1683]

To make Almond Butter:
The Lady Desmond's Receipt

Take a quart of creame and a quarter of a pound of Almonds blanched, beat them fine with a little of the creame to keep them from oyeling, then strayne them into the creame, and let it boyle, then put in the yolks of ten eggs well beaten and let it boyle till it curdles, then put it into a cloath and let the whay run from it, then take it out of the cloath and season it with rose, or orin_ge flower water, and sugar to your taste, bruise it with a spoone that it may looke smooth. [*Rebecca Price's Receipt Book,* 1681, in *The Compleat Cook,* ed. M. Masson, London, 1974]

1 pint (575 ml) double cream

2 oz (50 g) ground almonds
5 egg yolks
2 tbs (30 ml) caster sugar
2 tbs (30 ml) rosewater or orangeflower water

Liquidise the almonds with a little of the cream, then adding the remainder of the cream and the egg yolks. Bring the mixture to the boil, when it will form a curd. Strain through a cloth and liquidise the curd with the sugar and rosewater.

Fools

Fools, meanwhile, were made by thickening a fruit purée with eggs, these dishes being popular throughout the medieval period:

To make an Apple Moise

Roste your Apples very faire, and when you have so doon, peele them and strain them with the yolk of an Egge or twaine, and Rosewater, and boile it on a Chefing-dish of Coles with a peece of sweet Butter, put in sugar and ginger, and when you lay it in your dish, cast sinamon and Sugar on it. [A.W., *A Book of Cookrye*, 1587, (36)v]

1½ lb (700 g) cooking apples
2 egg yolks
2 tbs (30 ml) rosewater
2 tbs (30 ml) sugar
1 oz (25 g) butter
pinch of ginger, cinnamon for decoration

Core the apples, and bake at gas mark 6, 400°F (200°C) for 45–60 minutes, until soft. Scoop out the pulp, blend with the beaten egg yolks, sugar, butter, and ginger, and cook until thick. Pour into a serving dish, allow to cool, and sprinkle with cinnamon and a little sugar.

Gooseberry fool may be made in the same manner, the fruit being simmered to tenderness, for about 10 minutes, and drained before being blended.

Dishing The stiffer creams, such as Piramidis Cream or Spanish

Papps, were moulded in wine glasses, while ice-cream was turned out of its metal mould directly onto a shallow dish. Syllabubs were served in specially designed individual glass vessels with straight sides, small handles, and a small spout from which the alcoholic whey could be drunk from beneath the rich firm curd. The majority of the creams were served in glass, 'china', or silver basins, contemporary cooks advising that 'the broader your cream-bason is, the more beautifull your cream will look'. Alternatively, Rebecca Price recommended that her Spannish Cream should be 'putt on a silver salver in spoonefulls and it will keepe in single spoonefulls without running together'.

Some of the recipes suggested that the creams could be decorated by being sprinkled with sugar and spices, while others had small 'seeds' or knots tied in long thin strips of orange or lemon peel spread across their surface.

Before commercially prepared gelatine became available, **Jelly and leach** each houshold had to prepare its own as and when required, using either calf's foot or shavings of antler called hartshorn. These were boiled for hours before being strained and clarified:

> To make an excellent Jelly
>
> Take three gallons of fair water, boil in it a knuckle of veal and two calves' feet slit in two with all the fat clean taken from between the claws, so let them boil to a very tender jelly, keeping it clean skimmed and the edges of the pot always wiped with a clean cloth, that none of the scum may boil in them. Strain it from the meat and let it stand all night, and the next day take away the top and the bottom, and take to a quart of this jelly half a pint of sherry sack, half an ounce of cinnamon and as much sugar as will season it, six whites of eggs very well beaten; mingle all these together, then boil it half an hour and let it run through your jelly bag. [Joan Cromwell, *The Court*

and Kitchen of Elizabeth commonly called Joan Cromwell,
1664, p.134]

$^3/_4$ pt (425 ml) water
$^1/_2$ oz (15g) gelatine
1 tbs (15 ml) cinnamon
$^1/_4$ pt (150 ml) dry sherry
2 tbs (30 ml) sugar
1 lightly beaten egg white

Dissolve the gelatine in the boiling water, and allow to cool. Add the remainder of the ingredients and boil in a large pan for a few minutes before straining through a jelly bag.

Alternatively, replace the cinnamon and sherry with half a teaspoon (2.5 ml) each of ground ginger, nutmeg and mace, and the juice of two lemons, as advised by Rebecca Price. (For hartshorn jelly, see the Piramidis Cream recipe, p. 78.)

Coloured Jelly

If you would have your jelly of Harts-horne off severall coulers you must, when you have gott it redy to the sweetening, instead of the lofe sugar put in sirrup of clovegilliflower enough to sweeten it and couller it to your likeing; which will make it a fine red; and for blue, sweeten another part of it with sirrup of violets, which will give a fine couller, and for yellow you may dye it with saffarn as yellow as you would have it; ... you may put your jelly into glaces and the severall coullers will looke well throuw them also. [*Rebecca Price's Receipt Book*, 1681]

Today, it is more convenient to use red, violet and yellow food colourings to dye the jelly; or claret could replace the sherry in the recipe for 'an excellent jelly' (as advised in W.M.'s *Compleat Cook* of 1671, p.119).

Leach

This unusual dish has a delicious cool, sweet flavour and a translucent ivory-white appearance, being somewhat similar to Turkish delight, but much less cloying to the palate.

A white leach

Take a quart of newe milke, and three ounces weight of Isinglasse, halfe a pounde of beaten suger, and

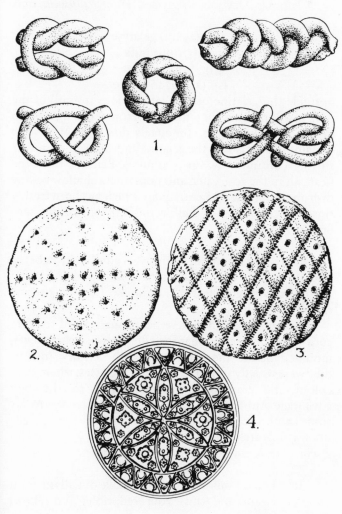

9.
Biscuits for the banquet; including knots or jumbles (1), cracknells (2), Shropshire cakes (3) and a wafer from a pair of sixteenth-century iron wafer-tongs (4).

1.

2.

3.

4.

stirre them together, and let it boile half a quarter of an hower till it be thicke, stirring them all the while: then straine it with three spoonfull of Rosewater, then put it into a platter and let it coole, and cut it in squares. Lay it fair in dishes, and lay golde upon it. [Thomas Dawson, *The Good Huswifes Jewell*, 1596, p.19]

> 5 tsps (25 ml) gelatine
> 1 pt (575 ml) milk
> 4 oz (100 g) sugar
> 5 tsp (25 ml) rosewater

Sprinkle the gelatine onto 4 tablespoons (60 ml) of the milk in a cup. Leave for 5 minutes before standing the cup in hot water until it is completely dissolved. Warm the remaining milk, stir in the gelatine and sugar, and simmer, stirring continuously, for 5 minutes. Remove from the heat, stir in the rosewater, and pour into a shallow baking dish about 7 inches (15 cm) square which has been freshly rinsed in cold water, and allow to set before cutting into one-inch cubes.

Dishing Leach was either 'cutt out in slices', as advised by Rebecca Price, or cut into cubes and arranged neatly on dishes and decorated with gold leaf, as in Thomas Dawson's recipe for 'white leach'.

Although tin moulds were occasionally used to form curds into decorative shapes, jellies were rarely (if ever) moulded before the early eighteenth century. Instead, they were usually served in individual glasses, where their colour and transparency were shown to the best advantage. Ann Ingham's attractive alternative was to 'lay some Lemon Peele at ye bottome of your dish; and ye jelly upon it in careless lumps'.[7]

For a more interesting presentation, try:

Jelly Lemons

Take Lemon pills cutt in halves; take out all the meat very cleane, and whilst your [red, violet, and yellow]

jelly is hott pour it into the pills till you have filled
the halves; so let them stand till they are cold; then
cut them into quarters, the jelly and pills together,
and laye them on a silver server, and the severall
coullers mingled one among the others will look very
finely in ye lemon pills [*Rebecca Price's Receipt Book,
1681*]

Fruit tarts were usually made by baking raw fruits such as   **Tarts**
damsons, cherries, strawberries, gooseberries, apples, or
pears in covered pastry cases or 'coffins', flavouring them
with sugar, cinnamon, and ginger. More rarely, the fruits
could be pre-cooked, damsons being simmered on a plate
with rosewater; apples stewed, perhaps with wine; and
pears cooked in a sealed pot in the oven with a little water
and sugar, before being baked in open pastry cases.

The decoration of the lids of the tarts was of the greatest
importance, 'close it and carve it about the brims of the
dish as you please, prick it and bake it, scrape sugar upon
it' instructs Mrs Cromwell, when completing her 'dish of
apples'; while for her 'double Tart' she had a lid already cut
in floral designs and garnished with damson, raspberry,
apricot and cherry preserves, preserved quinces, and sugar
biscuits. From the late sixteenth century at least, it had
been customary to cut off the lid after the tart had been
baked, replacing it with an ornamental lid made of rich
puff paste.[8] A series of designs for these cut-laid tart lids
was published in Robert May's *Accomplisht Cook* of 1660,
each round bearing ornately cut and interlaced strips of
sugar-glazed pastry, the intervening spaces being filled
with preserves of contrasting colours before it was ready
to be placed on top of its tart.

To make a Tarte of Prunes

Take prunes and wash them, then boile them with
faire water, cut in half a penny loaf of white bread,
and take them out and strain them with Claret wine,
season it with sinamon, Ginger and Sugar, and a little

Rosewater, make the paste as fine as you can, and dry
it, and fill it, and let it drie in the oven, take it out and
cast on it Biskets and Carawaies. [A.W., *A Book of
Cookrye*, 1587, p.31]

Filling
12 oz (350 g) prunes
4 oz (100 g) fresh white breadcrumbs
½ pt (275 ml) red wine
1 tsp (5 ml) cinnamon
1 tsp (5 ml) ground ginger
4 oz (100 g) sugar
1 tbs (15 ml) rosewater
Pastry
3 oz (75 g) butter
4 oz (100 g) plain flour
1 tsp (5 ml) caster sugar
1 beaten egg

Soak the prunes overnight, then simmer in a little water
for 10–15 minutes until tender. To make the pastry, rub the
butter into the flour, mix in the sugar and slowly stir in the
egg until it forms a soft dough which can be lightly
kneaded with the hands. Roll out the pastry and use to line
an 8 inch (20 cm) diameter, 2 inch (5 cm) deep flan ring.
Line the pastry with greaseproof paper, fill with uncooked
haricot beans or crusts, and bake blind at gas mark 7, 425°F
(220°C) for 15 minutes, then remove the beans and paper,
etc.

For the filling drain and stone the prunes, then blend
them with the remaining ingredients to form a smooth
thick paste. Spoon the filling into the pastry case, return to
the oven, and bake at gas mark 4, 350°F (180°C) for 1½
hours.

How to make an Almond Tart
Rise an excellent good paste with six corners, an inch
deep, take some blanched almonds very finely beaten
with rose-water. Take a pound of sugar to a pound of
almonds, some grated nutmeg, a little cream, with

strained spinach as much as will colour the almonds green, so bake it with a gentle heat in an oven, not shutting the lid, draw it, and stick it with candied orange and citron, and red and white muscadine. [Joan Cromwell, *The Court and Kitchen of Elizabeth, commonly called Joan Cromwell*, 1664, p.131]

> 11 oz (300 g) ground almonds
> 11 oz (300 g) sugar
> ¼ pt (150 ml) cream
> pinch of ground nutmeg
> green food colouring
> pastry case (made as in the previous recipe)

Mix the ingredients to a smooth paste, and bake in the case at gas mark 1, 275°F (140°C) for 20 minutes.

To make Cheesecakes

Take a good morning milk cheese, or better, of some eight pound weight, stamp it in a mortar, and beat a pound of butter amongst it, and a pound of sugar, then mix with it beaten mace, two pound of currans well picked and washed, a penny manchet grated, or a pound of almonds blanched and beaten fine with rose-water, and some salt, then boil some cream, and thicken it with six or eight eggs, mixed with the other things, work them well together, and fill the cheesecakes, make the curd not too soft, and make a paste of cold butter and water according to these forms. [Robert May, *The Accomplisht Cook*, 3rd edn, 1671, p.291]

> 8 oz (200 g) curds or cottage cheese,
> rubbed through a sieve
> 1 oz (25 g) butter
> 1 oz (25 g) sugar
> 2 oz (50 g) currants
> 1 oz (25 g) ground almonds
> 2 tbs (30 ml) cream, beaten with
> 1 egg yolk
> ¼ tsp (1.5 ml) ground mace

pinch of salt
pastry: as for 'Tarte of Prunes'
Cream the butter and sugar, and mix in the remainder of
the ingredients. Divide the pastry into two and roll these
out into large rounds. Place one of these on a baking sheet
and lay a thick layer of the mixture across it to within half
an inch of the edge. Using a fork, a skewer, and the back of
a knife, prick and mark the other sheet with one of the
given designs, place it over the mixture and seal the
moistened edges of the two sheets of pastry together.
Brush the top with either egg white or a mixture of caster
sugar, rosewater, and melted butter, and bake at gas mark 7,
425°F (220°C) for 15 minutes, then reduce the heat to gas
mark 4, 350°F (180°C) for a further 10 minutes.

Biscuits and wafers Although cakes rarely formed part of the banquet, various
forms of light sponge biscuit played an important role,
since they provided an excellent crisp, delicate, and bland
foil to all the rich fruit- and sugar-based dishes which
formed the bulk of this course.

Most biscuits were first baked in the oven, and then
returned to the oven once more, perhaps after the bread
had been withdrawn, in order to dry out completely, this
process recalling the origins of biscuits as 'twice-cooked
bread'. One of the earliest varieties was called biscuit-
bread, this being made by baking a yeast or egg-raised loaf
in either a rectangular baking-tin or in the form of a long
roll. When cool, it was cut in slices, sugared, and dried in
the oven like a rusk, after which it would be boxed up and
kept ready for use:

To make fine bisket bread
Take a pound of fine flower, and a pound of sugar,
and mingle it together, a quarter of a pound of
Anniseedes, foure eggs, two or three spoonfuls of
Rosewater put all these into an earthen panne. And
with a slyce of Wood beate it the space of twoo
houres, then fill your moulds halfe full: your

mouldes must be of Tinne, and then lette it into the oven, your oven beeing so whot as it were for cheat bread, and let it stande one houre and a halfe: you must annoint your moulds with butter before you put in your stuffe, and when you will occupie of it,

10.
Dating from the late seventeenth century, these moulds, carved in shallow detail in fine-grained wood, were used to produce the ornate gilded gingerbreads of the period.

slice it thinne and dry it in the oven, your oven beeing no whotter then you may abide your hand in the bottome. [Thomas Dawson, *The Good Huswife's Jewell*, 1596, p.13]

4 oz (100 g) plain flower

4 oz (100 g) caster sugar

1 oz (25 g) aniseed

2 eggs

2 tsp (10 ml) rosewater

Beat the egg white to stiffness, then beat the egg yolk, and slowly beat in the caster sugar, fold in the flour, and finally the aniseed and rosewater. Put the mixture into a greased and floured loaf tin, and bake for 25 minutes at gas mark 4, 350°F (180°C). When cold, cut the loaf into thin slices and dry in the oven on the lowest setting for 10 minutes.

Various other sponge-textured biscuits became popular during the seventeenth-century — the Naples biscuits, Italian biscuits, Prince biscuits, drop biscuits, almond biscuits, lemon biscuits, shell-bread, etc. — all made from combinations of fine flour, sugar, eggs, and various flavourings. In addition, there were both cracknells and jumbals, which had originally been plunged into a pan of boiling water, from which, after a short time, they rose to the surface, were caught in a skimmer and only then transferred to the oven. By the seventeenth century, however, the boiling process had been largely abandoned.

To make Cracknels

Take half a pound of fine flour dryed and searced, as much fine sugar searced, mingle with a spoonful of Coriander-seed bruised, half a quarter of a pound of Butter rubbed in the flour and sugar, then wet it with the yolk of two Eggs, and half a spoonful of white Rose-water, a spoonful or little more of Cream as will wet it; knead the Past till it be soft and limber to rowl well, then rowl it extream thin, and cut them round by little plates; lay them upon buttered Papers, and when they go up into the Oven, prick them, and wash the top with the yolk of an Egg beaten, and made thin with Rose-water or fair water; they will give with keeping, therefore before they are eaten, they must be dryed in a warm oven to make them crisp. [W.M., *The Compleat Cook*, 1671 edn, p.40]

4 oz (100 g) flour
4 oz (100 g) caster sugar
1 tsp (5 ml) ground coriander
3 tbs (45 ml) rosewater
1 oz (25 g) butter
1 tbs (15 ml) cream
2 egg yolks

Rub the butter into the flour, sugar and coriander, and make into a dough with the cream, one egg yolk, and one tablespoon of rosewater. Roll out thinly, place on a baking sheet, prick all over, and glaze with the remaining egg yolk and rosewater lightly beaten together. Bake for 10 minutes at 350°F (180°C).

To make Knots or Gumballs,
take 12 yolks of Egges, & 5 Whites, a pound of searced Sugar, half a pound of Butter washed in Rose Water, 3 quarters of an ounce of Mace finely beaten, a little Salt dissolved in Rose Water, half an ounce of Caroway-seeds, Mingle all theise together with as much Flower as will worke it up in paste, & soe make it Knotts or Rings or What fashion you please. Bake them as Bisket-bread, but upon Pye-plates. [Henry Fairfax; *Arcana Fairfaxiana manuscripta,* facsimile edn., 1980, p.65]

1½ oz (40 g) butter
1 tbs (15 ml) rosewater
4 oz (100 g) sugar
2 eggs, beaten
1 tsp (5 ml) ground mace
1 tsp (5 ml) aniseed
1 tsp (5 ml) caraway seed
8 oz (225 g) flour

Beat the butter with the rosewater; then cream with the sugar. Mix in the beaten eggs and spices, then work in the flour to make a soft dough. Make into long rolls about $\frac{1}{4}$ inch (5 mm) in diameter, and form into knots, rings, or plaited strips, etc., before baking on a lightly greased baking sheet for 15–20 minutes, at gas mark 4, 350°F (180°C).

Shortcakes were made too, the most popular being the Shropshire or Shrewsbury cakes variously flavoured with minced ginger, cinnamon, cloves, or nutmeg.

To make a Shropsheere cake

Take two pound of dryed flour after it has been searced fine, one pound of good sugar dried and searced, also a little beaten sinamon or some nottmegg greeted and steeped in rose water; so straine two eggs, whites and all, not beaten to it, as much unmelted butter as will work it to a paste: so mould it & roule it into longe roules, and cutt off as much at a time as will make a cake, two ounces is enough for one cake: then roule it in a ball between your hands; so flat it on a little white paper cut for a cake, and with your hand beat it about as big as a cheese trancher and a little thicker than a paste board: then prick them with a comb not too deep in squares like diamons and prick every cake in every diamon to the bottom; so bake them in a oven not too hot: when they rise up white let then soake a little, then draw. If the sugar be dry enough you need not dry but searce it: you must brake in your eggs after you have wroat in some of your butter into your flower: prick and mark them when they are cold: this quantity will make a dozen and two or three, which is enough for my own at a time: take off the paper when they are cold. [Madame Susan Avery, *A Plain Plantain: Country Wines, Dishes and Herbal Cures from a 17th-century Household MS Receipt Book,* ed. R. G. Alexander, 1922]

8 oz (225 g) butter
1 lb (450 g) flour
8 oz (225 g) caster sugar
¼ tsp (1.5 ml) grated nutmeg
1 egg
1 tsp (5 ml) rosewater

Rub the butter into the dry ingredients, then work in the egg and rosewater to form a very stiff dough. Cut off lumps of the dough and work into ¼ inch (5 mm) thick circles, 4 inches (10 cm) in diameter. Using a comb, mark the top surface into diamonds, cutting halfway through the cake, then use a broad skewer to prick through the centre of each diamond. Transfer to baking sheets, and bake for 20 minutes at gas mark 4, 350°F (180°C). Remove from the sheets with a metal spatula and place on a wire tray to cool.

Wafers

Wafers were thin discs of delicately flavoured biscuit made by squeezing a spoonful of rich batter between the lightly buttered faces of a pair of specially designed iron tongs which had been pre-heated over the fire.

To make Waffers

Take a pd. of fine flower boulted two or three times over, five or six spoonfulls of Cream, the Yolks of four Eggs, & seven or Eight spoonfulls of very good Rose-Water, beat all these together very well, then strain them thro a Strayner. Season them with Salt and Sugar till they tast very well. Your Irons that they bake them in must not bee too Hott that they bake white, & when they are ready to be taken from the fire, rowl them upon a round Stick the Bigness of your finger, and so let them stand near the fire, that they may be keep't Hard & Dry, add as much fair watter as Rose watter. [Frances Elsley ms printed in P. Brears, *The Gentlewoman's Kitchen*, Wakefield, 1984, p.75]

2 egg yolks
⅛ pt (75 ml) cream

⅛ pt (75 ml) rosewater
⅛ pt (75 ml) water
8 oz (225 g) flour

Slowly beat the flour into the liquids, adding sufficient additional water to produce a creamy mixture, similar to a pancake batter. Heat both faces of the irons evenly, pour a pool of batter onto one face and quickly clamp the irons together. The batter rapidly expands to fill the space between the irons, forcing the surplus out around the edges, where it may be trimmed off with a knife. At this stage the wafer begins to whine, as small spurts of delightful rose-scented steam are emitted. Return the irons to the heat, heating both sides to cook the wafer evenly. After a minute or two, the irons may be opened and the wafer removed by rolling it around the handle of a wooden spoon. If the wafer is soft and sticks to both faces, it is still uncooked.

Wafers cooked in this way were placed around dishes of cream, sweet butters, 'Spannish Papps', etc., with which they were eaten.

Gingerbreads Unlike today's gingerbreads, which are really a variety of sweet ginger-flavoured sponge-cake, those served at Tudor and Stuart banquets were dense dough-like pastes which could be shaped in shallow wooden moulds, dried to firmness, and finally gilded with gold leaf. The combination of spices used to give them flavour usually results in an interesting, warm, gentle taste in the front of the mouth, but this may conceal a strong bite of ginger, which, arriving some seconds later, can bring tears to the eyes of the unwary. There were two main varieties: the red, based on a dough of dried breadcrumbs and red wine; and the white, based on gum-reinforced icing sugar, perhaps with addition of ground almonds:

To make [red] Gingerbread

Take three stale Manchets and grate them, drie them, and sift them through a fine sieve, then adde unto them one ounce of ginger beeing beaten, and as much Cinamon, one ounce of liquorice and aniseedes being beaten together and searced, halfe a pound of sugar, then boile all these together in a posnet, with a quart of claret wine till they come to a stiffe paste with often stirring of it; and when it is stiffe, mold it on a table and so drive it thin, and print it in your moldes: dust your moldes with Cinamon, Ginger and liquorice, beeing mixed together in fine powder. This is your gingerbread, used at the Court, and in all gentlemens houses at festival times. It is otherwise called drie Leach. [Sir Hugh Platt, *Delightes for Ladies*, 1609, A22]

8 oz (225 g) fresh white breadcrumbs
1 tsp (5 ml) ground ginger
1 tsp (5 ml) cinnamon
1 tsp (5 ml) aniseed
1 tsp (5 ml) ground liquorice (if available)
1 oz (25 g) sugar
$\frac{1}{4}$ pt (150 ml) claret

Dry the breadcrumbs under the grill or in the oven (but without browning), and work them with the remaining ingredients in a saucepan over a low heat until it has become a stiff dough. Turn it out on to a board dusted with ground ginger and cinnamon, knead, and roll out to about $\frac{1}{4}$ inch (5 mm) in thickness. It may then be impressed with a small stamp, such as a butter-print, and cut out with a pastry cutter. Alternatively, it may be pressed into gingerbread moulds dusted with finely ground ginger and cinnamon. Trim off the surplus with a knife, invert the mould, and tap the end gently on the table top to knock out the print. The gingerbreads may then be laid on a wire rack to dry.

To make White Gingerbread

Take Gumma Dragagantis halfe an ounce, and steep it in rosewater two daies, then put thereto a pound of Sugar beaten & finely serced, and beate them well together, so that it may be wrought like paste, then role it thin into two Cakes, then take a fewe Jordain almonds and blaunch them in colde water, then dry them with a faire Cloth, and stampe them in a morter very finelye, adding therto a little rosewater, beat finely also the whitest Sugar you can get and searce it.

11.
Hand-blown glasses were used to display sweetmeats on the banquet table: the larger glass, about 6 ins high (1) was used for wet suckets, *c.* 1680; and the smaller, about 4$\frac{1}{2}$ ins high (2) for dry suckets, *c.* 1700. Lemons were cut with notched peels for inclusion in lemon salads (3), while stiff marmalades were modelled as oak leaves (4) or plums (5), each of the latter perhaps having a real stalk pushed into its body.

Then take Ginger, pare it and beat it very small and serce it, then put in sugar to the almonds & beat them togither very well, then take it out and work it at your pleasure, then lay it even upon one of your cakes, and cover it with an other and when you put it in the molde, strewe fine ginger both above and beneath. [A.W., *A Book of Cookrye*, 1587, p.37]

                1 tbs (15 ml) gelatine
                2 tbs (30 ml) rosewater
                1 lb (450 g) icing sugar
                8 oz (225 g) almond paste
                2 tsp (10 ml) ground ginger
                2 tsp (10 ml) ground cinnamon

Knead the spices into the almond paste and roll out into a rectangle about 1/8 inch (3 mm) in thickness. Mix the gelatine with the rosewater in a mug, and place it in boiling water until they have melted together. Sift the icing sugar into a bowl, and work the gelatine into it with a fork to form a stiff dough. Knead this to smoothness, dusting with cornflour to prevent it sticking to the board or the hands; divide in two, and roll each piece out to the same size as the almond paste. Place the almond paste between the two rectangles of sugar paste, and roll together to slightly over 1/8 inch (3 mm) thick, and print in moulds as above. Allow to dry on a wire rack.

The result is the purest white gingerbread enclosing a richly flavoured almond core.

Suckets and marmalades

Sweetmeats composed of fruit preserved with sugar formed one of the most important elements of the banquet, their colourful and flavoursome character reflecting the ladies' skilful work in the stillroom. Although most sugar-boiling techniques had been discovered by the late sixteenth century, their widespread use appears to have followed in the wake of the more plentiful supplies of this most expensive commodity which were being imported from the English colony of

Barbados from the 1640s. Many later seventeenth-century recipe books include detailed instructions in sugar-boiling, giving the impression that this was a new addition to the provincial cook's repertoire:

> To know how to clarify your Sugar
>
> R. a pint of fair water, & beat the whites of an Egge in itt, to froth; then putt a pound of sugar into itt, & lett itt boyle very fast, and there will rise a black foame on the toppe of itt, & when itt riseth, take itt off very clean, & when the Syrrup is very clear, strain through a cloth, & soe use itt as the Receit following doth direct you.
>
> To know when your Sugar is att a Candy-height
>
> R. your Sugar, & clarify itt as the preceding Receit doth direct you; Lett itt boyle againe & let itt boyle till itt draw betwixt your fingers in great flakes like your bird-lime, & soe you may use itt as the following Receit doth direct you.
>
> To know when your Sugar is att a casting height
>
> When your Sugar is clarified, as the first Receit does direct you, sett itt to boyle, till itt boyle thick, then stirre itt sometimes with a stock or a spoone, & when you stirre itt swing your stick from you, & when itt is att a casting height, your Sugar will flie from your stock, in great flakes of snow, or like Feathers flying in the aire, & soe you may use itt. (If you stirre itt with a spoone, you must swing your spoone from you, as you do the stock). [*Margaret Savile's Recipe Book,* 1683]

The methods by which sweetmeats were made varied enormously, as the hundreds of surviving manuscript and printed recipes show. Those which follow have been selected to illustrate their major types, all being reproducable today.

Perhaps the simplest of sweetmeats were made by slicing the fruit and sprinkling it with sugar:

To make a Sallet of Lemmons
Cut out slices of the peele of the Lemmons long
waies, a quarter of an inche one peece from another,
and then slice the Lemmon very thinne and lay him
in a dish crosse, and peeles about the Lemmons, and
scrape a good deale of suger upon them, and so serve
them. [Thomas Dawson, *The Good Huswifes Jewell*,
1596, p.26]

Succade, later anglicised to sucket, was made by boiling
orange or lemon peels in changes of water to remove most
of their bitterness, after which they were simmered in a
honey or sugar syrup. In the early sixteenth century, it was
being imported from Southern Europe, but the English
housewives soon learnt how to make it for themselves:

To make sucade of peeles of Lemmons
First take off your peeles by quarters and seeth them
in faire water, from three quartes to three pintes, then
take them out, and put to as much more water, and
seeth them likewise, and doo againe, till the water
wherein they are sodden have no bitterness at all of
the peeles, then you are ready, now prepare a Sirop
[of] the same liquor... one pint of rosewater, and for
every quart of liquor one half pound of sugar; seethe
them againe together on a soft fire of coles till the
Sugar bee incorporated with the liquor, then put in
your peeles, let them seeth softly till you percieve
that your sirop is as thicke as lite hony. Put them in a
pot of stone. [John Partridge, *The Treasurie of
Commodious Conceits, and Hidden Secrets*, 1573]

3 lemons
2 tbs (30 ml) rosewater
14 oz (400 g) sugar

Halve the lemons, squeeze out the juice (use this for some
other purpose), cut the rinds into quarters, and scrape out
any remaining membranes. Boil the rinds in 1 pt of water
for 30 minutes, changing the water three times during this
period so that no bitter taste remains and they are very

tender. Make a syrup with the sugar, rosewater, and ¾ pt (425 ml) of the water from the last boiling, and simmer the peels in this until they are translucent and the syrup is as thick as thin honey. Store in sterilised jars until required. Orange peel may also be prepared in this way.

Being in syrup, these were known as wet suckets. Other fruits were also preserved in a similar manner, as demonstrated in the following recipes:

The best way to Preserve Apricocks

Take the weight of your Apricocks, what quantity soever you mind to use, in Sugar finely beaten, pare and stone the Apricocks, and lay them in the Sugar, in your preserving pan all night, and in the morning set them upon hot embers till the Sugar be all melted, then let them stand, and scale an hour, then take them off the fire, and let them stand in that Syrupe two dayes, and then boyle them softly till they be tender and well coloured, and after that when they be cold put them up in glasses or pots, which you please.

[*A Book of Fruits and Flowers*, 1653, p.36]

1 lb (450 g) apricots, pared and stoned
1 lb (450 g) sugar

As the apricots are pared, put them in the sugar in a stainless pan and leave them there, in a cool place overnight, then place over the very lowest heat for an hour, stirring gently until the sugar is all melted. Skim the syrup clean and leave the apricots and syrup for two days, then re-heat, skim once more, pour into sterilised jars and seal.

The apricots or any other similar fruit preserved in this way are rich in colour and flavour, and may be served with their clear, succulent syrup.

To conserve wardens all the yeere in sirrop

Take your wardens and put them into a great Earthen pot, and cover them close, set them in an Oven when you have set in your white bread, & when you have drawne your white bread, and your pot, & that they be so colde as you may handle them, then pill the thin skinne from them over a pewter dish, that you may save all the sirroppe that falleth from them: put to them a quarte of the same sirroppe, and a pinte of Rosewater, and boile them together with a fewe Cloves and Sinnamon, and when it is reasonable thick and cold, put your wardens and Sirroppe into a

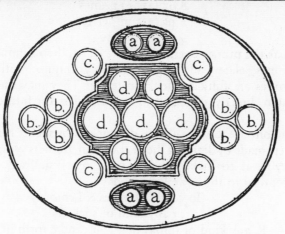

12.
This elevation and plan of the banquet table, showing its geometric layout and high pyramids of sweetmeats, comes from Massialot's *New Instructions for Confectioners* first published in France in 1692, and in England ten years later. In 1723 John Nott copied it almost precisely in his *Cook's & Confectioner's Dictionary:* small pyramids on two china dishes (a), little cups of iced waters (b), compotes (c), preserved and raw fruits in season (d).

Galley pot and see alwaies that the Syrrop bee above the Wardens, or any other thing that you conserve. [*The Second Part of The Good Huswives Jewell*, 1597, p.38]

> 3 lb (1.4 kg) pears
> 1½ pt (850 ml) water
> 8 oz (225 g) sugar
> ¼ pt (150 ml) rosewater
> 1 tsp (5 ml) whole cloves
> 2 sticks cinnamon

Place the pears in a casserole and bake at gas mark 4, 350°F (180°C) for 1–1½ hours until soft to the touch. Cool, then peel. Simmer any liquor which runs from them with a syrup made from the remaining ingredients, add the pears, and simmer for a few minutes before cooling.

To make Prunes in Sirrope

Take Prunes, and put Claret Wine to them, and Sugar, as much as you thinke will make them pleasant, let all these seeth together till yee thinke the Liquor looke like a sirrope, and that your Prunes be well swollen; and so keepe them in a vessel as yee doe greene Ginger. [J. Partridge, *The Treasurie of Commodious Conceites and Hidden Secrets*, 1573]

> 8 oz (225 g) prunes
> ¾ pt (425 ml) claret
> 4 oz (100 g) sugar

Soak the prunes overnight in the claret, then simmer the prunes, claret, and sugar for 10–15 minutes until the prunes are fully swollen and tender. They may then be eaten directly, or sealed in sterilised jars for future use.

In contrast to wet suckets, dry suckets or sucket candies were made by draining the peel, or fruit, from its syrup and drying it to make candied peels or crystallised fruits identical to those we know today:

To candy Oranges & Lemons,
or any kind of sucketts

R. any kind of things that you candie forth of their

syrrup after they are preserved, & wash their syrrup clean from them in water, & dry them, then clarify your sugar & candy itt to a manner chrystal [Manus Christi] height, & put as many sucketts into itt as your syrrup will cover, & let boyle till your sugar is att a casting height, then sett them to coole, & when the syrrup begins to coole, take them forth & when they are cold they will be candied white and cleane. [*Margaret Savile's Recipe Book*, 1683]

8 oz (225 g) sugar
¼ pt (150 ml) water

Take the orange or lemon peels prepared as in recipe for 'sucade of peeles of Lemmons', wash the syrup from them, dry them, and boil gently in a syrup made from the above ingredients boiled to around 220°F. Remove, drain, and cool on wire racks. (For details of sugar-boiling, see *The Constance Spry Cookery Book*, 1967 edn. pp.857–60.)

Marmalades

Stiff pastes of sugar and fruit pulp were made firm enough to be cut into squares or modelled into decorative shapes. These included the chardequynce and condiniac of the medieval English kitchen, and the marmalades later imported from the countries of Southern Europe, all of which originally used quinces as their main ingredient. Many of the later recipes used other fruits in a similar manner: apricots, oranges, lemons, peaches, and pippins all being popular. The fascinating story of these and similar preserves is given in C. Anne Wilson's *The Book of Marmalade* (1985).

Sucket candies

To make marmalade of Lemmons or Oranges Take the Lemmons or Oranges and boyle them with halfe a dozen pippins, and so drawe them through a strainer then take so much sugar as the pulp doth weigh ... and boxe it up. [Sir Hugh Platt, *Delightes for Ladies*, 1609, A41]

5 large lemons or oranges
3 apples (e.g. Cox's pippins)

¼ pt (150 ml) water
about 1 lb (450 g) sugar

Quarter the lemons and remove the pips, stalk, etc., while holding them over a stainless steel pan to catch the juice. Peel, core, and quarter the apples, and simmer gently with the lemons and water for 45–60 minutes, until tender. Remove from the heat and either rub through a sieve or blend to a smooth paste. Weigh the pulp, add its weight of sugar, and stir over a low heat until very stiff. It may then be turned on to a lightly greased plate, worked into a shallow square block and allowed to cool.

Sweet-Meats of my Lady Windebanks

She maketh a past of Apricocks (which is both very beautiful and clear, and tasteth most quick of the fruit) thus. Take six pound of pared and sliced Apricocks, put them in a high pot, which stop close, and set it in a kettle of boiling water, till you perceive the flesh is all become a uniform pulp; then put it out into your preserving pan or possenet, and boil it gently till it be grown thick, stirring it carefully all the while. Then put two pound of pure Sugar to it, and mingle it well, and let it boil gently, till you see the matter come to such a thickness and solidity, that it will not stick to a plate. Then make it up into what form you will. The like you may do with Raspes or Currants. [Sir Kenelm Digby, *The Closet of Sir Kenelm Digby Opened*, 3rd edn. 1677, p.244]

8 oz (225 g) (when prepared)
peeled and stoned apricots
3 oz (75 g) sugar

Place the apricots in a heatproof jar, seal the top with a piece of cooking foil, and stand in a covered saucepan of boiling water for an hour. Pour the apricots into a small saucepan and gently boil, stirring continuously until the paste is extremely thick, then add the sugar and continue stirring. When it is so thick that it has to be spread across the bottom of the pan with a spoon, it may be turned on to a lightly greased plate, worked into a shallow square block, and allowed to cool. It has a deep orange colour, and is every bit as good today as Sir Kenelm found it three centuries ago.

If these marmalades were to be served immediately,

13.
The banqueters ate their sweetmeats from the plain backs of wafer-thin wooden trenchers painted and gilded with beautiful designs and popular verses. The silver sucket forks, combinations of a spoon and a fork, were ideally designed for these functions. The left-hand example dates from *c.* 1660; that on the right from the 1680s.

they were cut into small squares and piled on platters; if they were to be stored, they were moulded into specially made marmalade boxes — Lord Robert Dudley purchased 'a brick of marmalade, 2s, 4d [11½p]' for a banquet at Eltham in November 1560.

Alternatively, when the marmalade had been boiled so stiff that the spoon stood upright in it, the cook could either:

> take it up and lay it in a platter or charger in pretty lumps as big as you will have the moulds or prints, and when it is cold print it on a fair board with sugar: and print thereon a mould or what knot or fashion you will, and bake it in an earthen pot or pan upon the embers, or in a fair cover, and keep them continually by the fire to keep them dry. [A.W., *A Book of Cookrye*, 1587, p.42]

or

> fashion [it] on a Pye-plate, like Oaken leaves, and some like half Plums, the next day close the half Plums together; and if you please you may put the stones and stalks in them and dry them in an Oven, and if you will have them look green, make the [pippin] paste when the pippins are green; and if you would have them look red, put in a little of Conserves of Barberries in the Paste, and if you will keep any of it all the year, you must make it as thin as Tart stuff, and put it into Gallipots. [W.M., *A Queens Delight*, 1671 edn. p.63]

In contrast to these dense pastes, clear cakes of various fruits were almost transparent, their hard, boiled sugar base being given fruit flavours just as in today's fruit drops:

Drop cakes of Lemons

> Take the juce of Lemon one spoonfull and make it thike with fine lofe suger, and let it simber but not boyle; grate in ye peele of a Lemon also, then when it is enough, with the poynt of a knife drop it on sheets

of paper to drye. [*Rebecca Price's Receipt Book,* 1681]
Grated rind of a lemon
1 tbls (15 ml) strained lemon juice
4 tbls (60 ml) caster sugar

Dissolve the sugar in the lemon juice in a saucepan and
heat very gently until the syrup becomes clear, continue to
cook gently to a soft crack (around 290°F), before adding
the grated lemon rind. Remove from the heat and allow
any bubbles to subside before dropping small spoonfuls
either onto a piece of lightly greased and *extremely flat*
greaseproof paper, or onto a lightly greased area of clean
plastic-finished worktop, to form cakes 1 inch or less in
diameter.

The last method of preservation to be described here is
drying, in which the fruit was first simmered in a syrup to
increase its sugar content, after which it was slowly oven-
dried.

Dried fruits

To drie Cherries

R. of the fairest cherries you can gett, stalked, stone
them, to six pound of cherries you must take one
pound of sugar, soe put them in to a Pan without
water, scald them on the fire, then take them into an
earthen pan, & let them stand 2 or 3 days, then put
them into the pan, & warme them againe, then take
them off the fire, & let them stand two days in the
syrrup, then put them out one by one upon a sieve, &
so sett them in an oven or the sun two days till you
find them very dry, then take some fair water & let itt
just boyle, them let itt stand and coole a little, that
you can well endure your hand in itt, then put them
in to itt, rubbing them in your hands, then take & rub
them in a clean cloth, then lay them one by one upon
a sieve, then set them a drying, & when they are dry,
put them in Papers, between every laying of cherries
lay a paper, & so they will keep all the year. [*Margaret
Savile's Recipe Book,* 1683]

To dry cherries:

1 lb (450 g) stoned cherries
3 oz (75 g) sugar

Put the cherries and sugar in a non-staining pan without water, and heat gently until the cherries are just covered by the syrup. Cover and leave in a cool place for two days, then heat to boiling point for 1 minute, and return to the cool for two days more. Carefully remove each cherry from the syrup and arrange on a wire tray either in the sun for two days, or in an oven heated to gas mark 4, 350°F (180°C); the heat then being turned off and left with the door slightly ajar, repeating this two or three times until they resemble large raisins.

The wet suckets and fruits preserved in syrup were usually dished in gadrooned glass bowls, frequently mounted on pedestal bases, so that their fine colour and translucency could be shown off to greatest advantage on the table. Dry suckets, meanwhile, were piled in smaller hemispherical glasses raised on baluster stems.

Notes

1. Randle Holme, *The Academy of Armoury* (1688), III p.80.
2. M Lorwin, *Dining with William Shakespeare* (New York, 1976), p.388: and *Archaeologia*, 21, (1821), p.287.
3. C. A. Wilson *Food and Drink in Britain* (Penguin, 1984) p.48; 'W.M.', *A Queen's Delight* (1671 edn.), p.69; and Sir Hugh Platt, *Delightes for Ladies* (1609), p.18.
4. T. Dawson, *The Good Huswifes Jewell* (1596), p.40; and Platt, *Delightes for Ladies*, p.38.
5. Platt, *Delightes for Ladies*, p.13.
6. Sir Kenelm Digby, *The Closet of Sir Kenelm Digby Opened*, 3rd edn. (1677), p.113.
7. Rebecca Price, *The Compleat Cook*, ed, M. Masson (1974), p.170. Ann Ingham married Roger Price and was Rebecca Price's mother.
8. T. Dawson, *The Good Huswifes Jewell*, pp.18, 25.

5.

Bowers of Bliss: The Banquet Setting

JENNIFER STEAD

The origins of the banquet in England are to be found in the medieval ending of a grand meal with hippocras and wafers, in the imported French ceremony of the *voidée* or void (which was additional wine and spices given after the tables had been cleared), and in the increasing use of sweetmeats, once considered medicinal and digestive – all coming together in the time of the early Tudors to make a separate final sweet course.

Banqueting houses

The *voidée* is derived from the French *voider,* to clear the table but it also means to make empty, and so refers to the departure of guests and of those people leaving the Great Hall or Chamber who were not staying to sleep there; therefore the *voidée* refers to the final wine, spices, comfits, etc., taken before departing or retiring.[1]

C. Anne Wilson has pointed out that in *Le Ménagier de Paris* (1393), the bourgeois, after grace, take their *voidée* standing; in a very large household, after grace and while the servants eat, the company withdraws to another room and waits there until wine and spices are brought. It is most likely that these are also consumed standing. The household Ordinances of Edward IV (1461–83) state: 'The King never taketh a voyd of comfittes and other spices, but standing'.[2] Indeed, it seems it was customary both in France and England to stand for the *voidée*. The practice of standing may also be related to the practical points that

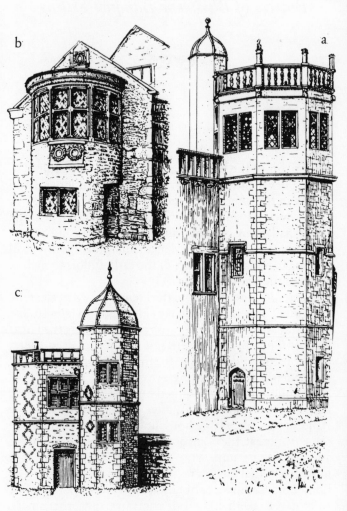

14(a)
Sir William Sharington's Tower, 1549–53, Lacock Abbey, Wiltshire. The two top rooms are for banqueting.

14(b)
Banqueting House at Barlborough Hall near Chesterfield, Derbyshire. The superb chimney-piece is dated 1587.

14(c)
Summer-cum-banqueting house, originally one of a pair, at Eyton-on-Severn, Shropshire, built 1607 for Sir Francis Newport.

15.
The stone table in the
top banqueting room,
Sir William
Sharington's Tower,
Lacock Abbey,
Wiltshire.

tables had to be cleared and dismantled to allow for after-dinner activities such as games and dancing, and that in very large households the only place where large numbers of servants could sit down to eat was the Great Hall (originally along with the lord and his family). But when there were many guests, the servants obviously could not eat at the same time, so that after a grand dinner it was necessary for the company to withdraw to another room after the hippocras and wafers, the handwashing and grace to allow the servants to sit at table. The *voidée* was taken in this withdrawing room, usually the Great Chamber, where the silver and plate were put on the cupboard for show.[3] A clear development can be seen: taking the void standing or walking about made the course already mobile and, when taken in another room, it became distinct from the main meal. It soon became easy to transport the *voidée* altogether as a separate sweet banquet to a totally removed place.

In England the comparative lateness of this separation of the sweet banquet course in the early sixteenth century coincided with a growing need for privacy and less ceremony.[4] In the thirteenth century lords ate in the Great Hall along with family and servants. From the mid-fourteenth century the lord and his family increasingly began to withdraw from the din, general confusion and time-consuming ritual to the Great Chamber, where, however, there were often still too many servants and too much ceremony. By the sixteenth century an even smaller, more private withdrawing chamber was used.[5] This need for intimacy, and the special easily transportable nature of sweet stuff, helped the transition to a separate banqueting course, which led, in turn, to the development of the separate banqueting house in the garden or on the roof, from where the servants could, if so desired, be dismissed entirely.

Only when they needed to impress with their wealth and position did the Court and great lords continue to

16.
The roofscape at Longleat House with turrets built *c.* 1569 by Robert Smythson for Sir John Thynne; the octagonal ones house stair heads, the rectangular ones are banqueting houses.

take the void/banquet in a large room or hall with the usual pomp and ceremony and lavish display of plate. When they did build separate banqueting houses, they were large and impressive. Some of the large banqueting houses, such as the royal banqueting house in Whitehall, could also be used for full meals. Some great houses had both a large banqueting house and a small private one (or more), as at Theobalds, Hardwick, Holdenby and Nonsuch.

After the battle of Bosworth in 1485, there was comparative peace, with no further need for fortified houses and curtain walls. Indeed, there was a craving in the early sixteenth century to look out over old confining high-walled gardens onto a wider world which was bound up with the growing Elizabethan appreciation of nature. This was possible only from the house roof or garden mount. Consequently, the prospecting house or banqueting house (they were usually one and the same thing) was built at such an elevation, giving deep spiritual and physical pleasure, as well as the added *frisson* of vertigo.

On a par with the conspicuous costliness of the sweetmeats, this setting of the banquet was of paramount importance — the Renaissance idea of the garden was as a paradise on earth, where senses, intellect and spirit were enhanced and sublimated. Renaissance gardens were set out as banquets for the mind, where one tasted a heightened sense of reality.

After a rich and heavy meal in the main house, diners would no longer be hungry, and so the nature of the banquet was not to satisfy the stomach, but to delight the eye. The banquet and banqueting house were designed to titillate and refresh, among birdsong, plashing water, fragrant flowers, and summer air, occasionally even in moonlight. Enchanting settings which distanced guests from the ordinary and familiar and gave them a newly awakened sense of self-awareness could be found also in purpose-built grottoes, water houses, fishing lodges, hunting lodges, towers, pavilions and belvederes: the more fanciful the better.

One of the first specific references to an outdoor banqueting house was in 1535, when Miles Coverdale mentions a banqueting house in such a way as to make it clear that it is separate from the house.[6] Wooden arbours in the garden and on tops of mounts from this time have not survived. These would most likely have been used for banqueting, as was the arbour on top of the mount in the Mount Garden at Hampton Court, erected in 1533–4. The South or Great Round Arbour was three storeys high, nearly all windows and with a lead-covered onion dome topped with a gilded crown and the king's beasts, giving delightful views onto the Privy Garden and onto the Thames.[7]

There was a similar banqueting house at Nonsuch. Nonsuch was Queen Elizabeth's favourite palace. Ten or twelve miles from London, between Cheam and Ewell, it was begun by her father, Henry VIII, in 1538. The banqueting house in the grounds was built on the highest hill in the park. Three storeys high, it was half-timbered, with round turrets at each corner, and a crowning lead-covered lantern. The main ground floor room was a hall, and there were eight more rooms, three and five, on the upper floors, all oak-panelled, with windows all round. On the top floor the turrets had balconies to view the scenery. Guests drinking wine or eating their 'banquetting stuffe' could certainly have wandered up to the turret balconies to view the countryside.[8]

It is not known whether Sir William Sharington had Nonsuch in mind or perhaps, something he had seen in his travels through France and Italy, when, between 1549 and 1553, he added on to his converted abbey at Lacock in Wiltshire an octagonal look-out tower. Such towers were fashionable in the mid-sixteenth century; but this had the startling novelty of two banqueting rooms, which still survive. The access to the lower room was through the rooms of the house, the upper one was accessible only from the roof, and is the earliest known banqueting house on a roof.[9] (Figure 14a)

Each room is very small and intimate, holding only six or seven people comfortably, though more guests could have attended the banquet, walking about on the roof. Both rooms have octagonal stone tables carved in Renaissance style: in the lower room the table is supported by four leering satyrs with baskets of fruit on their heads. This room has encaustic tile paving which includes the crest, arms, and initials of William Sharington. The banqueting rooms were by John

Chapman, the first English mason to understand thoroughly how to use the three classical orders accurately. (Figure 15.)

There were no real 'architects' in the modern sense of the word at this date. The aristocrat and gentleman tended to design their own houses, using French and Flemish pattern books (which were both after the Italian) with the help of skilled artificers like the Smythsons, the Thorpes, Lyminge and Chapman.

One of Sharington's guests, much impressed with this innovation, was Sir John Thynne who, in March 1568, began to build something similar at Longleat; this time not an externally appended tower, but four little banqueting houses on the roof approachable only from the roof itself. (Figure 16.) These were the earliest known work of Robert Smythson (the original idea may not have been his as they were conceived before his arrival, but the details are most likely his). Smythson came to work on the third Longleat House in March 1568, and his achievements included eight little turrets on the roof, called 'types' — four rectangular and four octagonal. These were to house the heads of the flights of stairs that ran up the angles of the courtyards to the roof. The specification stated:

> Item all the starres to Ryse above the howse and to be typed, and IIII to have lytle starres wonne fro the roofe so as they may serve as banketting howses.[10]

These four are the rectangular turrets, one of which still has 'lytle starres wonne fro the roofe'. The cupolas with scalecap domes and little arcaded lanterns seem to have been new in England, although it is possible they could have been influenced by other innovatory buildings which have since vanished.

It must have been delightful for Thynne and his guests to climb upwards and emerge as out of trapdoors onto the theatrical plane of the roof, to take in the air and superb views along with their wine and sweetmeats in a stage-managed and yet artless climax to a social occasion.

The miniature scale of these four banqueting houses would serve only to heighten the sensation of formidable grandeur in the distant prospect.

Smythson's roofscape at Worksop Manor, Nottinghamshire (he enlarged the house in the 1580s for the sixth Earl of Shrewsbury), is very much in the style of Longleat. The two round rooms in the lanterns were most likely prospecting or banqueting rooms.

Barlborough Hall, Derbyshire, whose owner, Sir Francis Rhodes, was patronised by the Earl of Shrewsbury, was built in 1683–4 in a style very close to that of Worksop, and was most likely also designed by Robert Smythson. To the west of the house there is a stone stable block with, attached to the south gable, a small banqueting house of two storeys with exterior access on both levels. A superb chimney-piece in the main upper room is dated 1587 (Figure 14b).

Robert Smythson also built Hardwick Hall, Derbyshire, for the Earl of Shrewsbury's wife, Bess of Hardwick, between 1590 and 1596, and its roof is also influenced by Longleat, perhaps directly or via Worksop. The roof is huge and flat, and the access is via a wide staircase in the north turret. In the south turret the top room, with its rich decorative plasterwork, is clearly a prospecting room or banqueting house from which the views were, and still are, breathtaking. There was also a banqueting house in the garden at Hardwick. The account books for the building of Hardwick Hall in 1596 detail the materials for 'the banqueting house in the garden'.[11]

Smythson also built a huge prospect room on the roof at Wollaton Hall, Nottingham, which could have been used for banquets. Another rooftop prospect room or banqueting house is in an octagonal cupola at Coleshill in Berkshire, built for Sir Roger Pratt between 1650 and 1662 with access to walkways on the leads.[12]

It will be seen that some banqueting houses were tiny, and others were quite big with multiple rooms. Sir

Christopher Hatton's banqueting house at Holdenby is such a one. It was built along with the mansion between 1580 and 1585 for a visit of Queen Elizabeth, though she never came. Only a hundred yards from Hatton's lavish mansion, it is three storeys high, with six rooms on each floor. It is, nevertheless, called a banqueting house and so must have been used for banqueting, as well as for lodging. At Holdenby there was also a little summer or banqueting house in the inner garden, on one of the four corner prospect mounts.[13]

Another who spent great sums on making his home fit to receive Queen Elizabeth was the Earl of Leicester, at Kenilworth Castle. The Queen's visit in 1575 is documented in detail by Robert Laneham, who describes the magnificent new aviary (probably used as a banqueting house) as being 'a cage sumptuous and beautiful' joined to the north wall of the castle, 30ft by 14ft and 20ft high, panelled, with columns, painted to look as if covered with diamonds, rubies, sapphires, and gold.[14]

One of the earliest extant drawings of a small garden banqueting house is the one done for Sir Henry Hobart of Blickling Hall, Norfolk, by Robert Lyminge, in the same style as the hall. (Lyminge, of foreign extraction, was 'surveyor' at Hatfield, one of the most impressive English houses.) In the drawing at Blickling, Lyminge used Renaissance motifs such as Hercules with his club, a crowning grenado, and other details out of Serlio's *Books of Architecture* (1559). On the plan he makes all sorts of suggestions such as: 'you may set statues on this buffet of stone as big as the lyfe or els they will make no shew'.[15] (Figure 17b)

There is a John Smythson drawing in the Royal Institute of British Architects (RIBA) of a banqueting house for Clifton Hall, Nottinghamshire, in the form of a 16ft square with little round rooms projecting from each corner (one contains a staircase), resulting in an octagonal central hall.[16] It was sited next to the bowling green—a not uncommon English juxtaposition, suggesting it had an extra function, as a refreshment room for bowlers. This was the case at Temple Newsam in Yorkshire. (Figure 18a)

A drawing by Robert Smythson in the RIBA depicts 'The Platforme of Lord Exeter's House at Wymbellton

17(a)
The East Banqueting House of the old manor of Camden, at Chipping Camden, Gloucestershire. The east and west banqueting houses were built three storeys high into the hillside at each end of the garden terrace for Sir Baptist Hicks in 1613.

17(b)
Projected banqueting house at Blickling Hall, Norfolk, taken from Robert Lyminge's drawing *c.* 1610–20, which uses details from Serlio's *Architecture*.

1609' and shows the banqueting house set in its sunken 85ft square in the formal garden not too far from the house.[17] There was also a wooden banqueting house at William Cecil's Wimbledon Hall at the east end of the long terrace.[18] It was fashionable to build paired banqueting houses at each end of a long terrace. (Figures 17a and 14c).

The designer of an amazing banqueting house at Cobham Hall, Kent, must surely have been the gardener, for it was actually made of a living tree. A lime had its lower branches interlaced into an arbour, then 8ft further up the trunk, branches were trained into a room with boards laid for a floor, and the same repeated 8 and 9 feet higher, again with stairs, making three rooms each holding 'half a hundred men'.[19] This example emphasises that garden banqueting houses belong essentially to garden design and not to house design.

Temporary banqueting houses could be made wholly of green and living stuff. Queen Elizabeth in the summer of 1560 gave a tournament for the entertainment of the French Embassy. She had had erected in Greenwich Park a banqueting house 'made with fir poles and decked with birch branches and all manner of flowers both of the field and of the garden; as roses, july flowers, lavender, marygolds and all manner of strewing herbs and rushes' wherein she gave a supper followed by a masque, and then a magnificent banquet.[20]

Some gentlemen designed their own gardens. Francis Bacon, philosopher and statesman, designed his own at Verulam House, St Albans, c.1608. In his essay 'Of Gardens' (1625) he describes another, the perfect princely garden. It is to be 30 acres, and divided into three parts: 'a Greene in the Entrance, a Heath or Desart in the Going forth; and the Maine garden in the midst; Besides Alleys, on both sides': He places his banqueting house on a 30ft mount:

I wish ... in the very Middle [of the main garden] a

Faire Mount, with three Ascents, and Alleys, enough for foure to walk abreast, which I would have to be Perfect Circles, without any Bulwarkes, or Imbosments; and the whole Mount, to be Thirty Foot high; And some fine Banquetting House, with some Chimneys neatly cast, and without too much Glasse.[21] (Figure 19).

Bacon's own garden differed somewhat from his imagined one. In the early years of the seventeenth century, he had built Verulam House, Gorhambury, St Albans's, at a cost of £9 000 to £10 000. Then, in 1621, he fell into disgrace and was fined £40 000 for corruption, whereupon his lavish life-style was reduced and he spent the rest of his life writing. In 1665–6 Verulam was in ruins, and was sold off for £400 to two carpenters. John Aubrey remembered seeing the house and garden in a ruined state in the 1650s, thirty years after Bacon's death:

— at severall good Viewes, were erected elegant Sommer-howses well built of Roman-architecture, well wainscotted and cieled; yet standing, but defaced, so that one would have thought the Barbarians had made a Conquest here.

There were 4 acres of fish-ponds. Aubrey goes on:

In the middle of the middlemost pond, in the Island, is a curious banquetting-house of Roman architecture, paved with black and white marble; covered with Cornish slatt, and neatly wainscotted.[22]

Bacon's summer houses were among the earliest examples in England of purely classical architecture.

The seventeenth century in England saw a plethora of books on gardening and garden design, prompted by the avalanche of innovations from Dutch and French gardening. Some of these books gave instructions on the building of a banqueting house on a mount as a focal point, for example, John Worlidge in 1681 advised the garden builder to use the waste earth left over from the excavation of ponds and ditches (canals) to raise a mount:

whereupon you may erect a Pleasure or Banquetting-
house or such like place of Repose ... Arbors, Benches
and Seats are very necessary . . . This small Edifice,
usually term'd a Pleasure-house or Banquetting-
house, may be at some remote Angle of your Garden;
For the more remote it is from your House, the more
private you will be from the frequent disturbances of
your Family and Acquaintance.[23]

John Worlidge is describing the banqueting house
on the mount towards the end of its period in fashion. In
another fifty years there would be no need to climb to a
height to see over walls and hedges to the countryside: the
ha-ha and the naturalistic landscape garden banished all
that, though banqueting houses continued to be built
throughout the eighteenth century, sited for the optimum
picturesque view.

It has been mentioned that the point at which some
bigger banqueting houses shaded into other designations,
such as lodge, is not always clear. In fact, many of the little
buildings used for banqueting were also used for a variety
of other activities. A very pragmatic one, that of gardener's
shed, is mentioned by John Rea, the gardener, in 1662,
when he stresses the need in a flower garden for:

a handsome Octagonal Somer-house, roofed in every
way, and finely painted with landskips, and other
conceits, furnished with seats about, and a Table in
the middle; which serveth not onely for delight and
entertainment, to sit in, and behold the beauties of
the Flowers, but for many other necessary purposes;
as, to put the Roots of Tulips, and other Flowers in, as
they are taken up, upon Papers, with the names upon
them, until they be dried.[24]

Another use was that of study or classroom. Sir William
Petre at Ingatestone Hall, Essex, had in the south-west
corner of his orchard, a banqueting house 'well and fair
builded'. 'In 1600, if not before, the upper floor of the
banqueting house included "a little study", probably for

the young heir; and "the schoolhouse chamber" may also have been under the same roof.'[25]

The need to pray, silently or aloud, away from the distractions of the house, made the banqueting house a perfect prayer room. At Callowden House in Warwickshire at the edge of a large pool a late sixteenth-century banqueting house was 'the polite work of the Lady Elizabeth, wife of Sir Thomas Berkeley . . . and the retired cell of her soul's soliloquies to God her creator'.[26] Sir Thomas Tresham, who built the Triangular Lodge at Rushton in Northamptonshire, was a Catholic, and built his fantastic 'conceit' between 1593 and 1596 as a prayer room cum summer house cum banqueting house. Having only three walls, the design is based with complicated mathematical and emblematic ingenuity on the number three, being a play on his name, the Trinity, etc.[27]

Hunting towers sometimes had dual uses. The hunting tower, or stand, at Walton Castle, on a height above the Bristol Channel near Walton-in-Gordano and now in ruins, embodies the romantic chivalric fashion for turrets and battlements about 1550:

> It is a perfect example of . . . a pageant fort made permanent in stone. Within an octagonal and embattled curtain wall with round towers at the angles is an octagonal central building decorated with cross-shaped arrow-slits. It was built by the first Lord Poulett in about 1615–20, probably as a stand or banqueting house.[28]

Another dual use was that of fishing lodge, sited near river or pond. There is a fishing/banqueting house at Hall in the Ponds, Sheffield, and another, dated 1591, was at Bourne Mill, Colchester.[29] A banqueting/fishing lodge was designed in 1570 by Sir Arthur Champernowne for his friend Richard Carew at Anthony, Cornwall, but was never realised. It was to have been built on an island in the saltwater pool below the house. The plan contained two little rooms and a little kitchen for fishing feasts:

The island was square, with round projections at each corner; the banqueting house had the same ground plan, but contained a round room within the square; above was a round turret containing a square room. There was a platform round the turret, and space for two rooms, for a little kitchen, a staircase, a store for fishing rods.[30]

The square and circle device was probably a delight in geometry for its own sake, though it could have been based on the philosophy of the harmonious plan of the universe.

An unusual banqueting house, with fish tanks and bathing facilities, was at William Cecil, Lord Burleigh's influential house at Theobalds. Theobalds was typically Elizabethan in its formal gardens, containing obelisks, columns, pyramids of stone and wood, topiary, canals with boats, labyrinths and fountains. Sir Paul Hentzner in 1598 describes it:

> After seeing these, We were led by the gardener into the Summer-house, in the lower part of which, built semi-circularly, are the twelve Roman Emperors, in white marble, and a table of touchstone; the upper part of it set round with cisterns of lead, into which water is conveyed through pipes, so that fish may be kept in them, and in summer time they are very convenient for bathing; in another room for entertainment, very near this, and joined to it by a little bridge, is an oval table of red marble.[31]

The black touchstone table in the Roman Emperor room was unusual: a solid piece, 8ft by 4ft, which left a streak when rubbed with gold or silver.

Banqueting within the sight and sound of water seems to have been particularly attractive. In 1583 Sir Philip Sidney recorded his visit to 'a banqueting-house among certain pleasant trees, where the table is set near to an excellent water-work'.[32] Many water houses, buildings which housed the pipes and pumps which supplied water

to both house and garden, served as banqueting houses.
At Kilkenny Castle in Ireland, the seat of the Duke of
Ormonde, this pragmatic but pretty arrangement was
described by Thomas Dineley in the time of Charles II.
Next to a bowling green was:

> a delightful water house ... which with an Engine of
> Curious Artifice by the help of one horse furnisheth
> all the offices of the Castle with that necessary
> Element. The Water house hath a pleasant Summer
> banqueting room, floor'd and lin'd with white and
> black marble, which abounds here, with a painted
> skye roof with Angells; in this is seen a fountaine of
> black marble in the shape of a large cup with a jet
> d'eau or throw of water ariseing mounts into the
> hollow of a Ducall Crown which but hangs over it,
> and descends again at severall droping places
> around.[33]

Other 'wettish' banqueting rooms were grottoes which
gave an enchanting underwater feeling. There is a fine one
in the gatehouse at Skipton Castle, Yorkshire, attributed
to Lady Anne Clifford, or her father. The room is lined in
volcanic stone, the architectural details described in ear
shells; the sun, Neptune, and cherubs all covered with
mother-of-pearl. Woburn Abbey has an impressive grotto
dated about 1627. It is 20ft square with one side opening
through three arches into the garden, and probably
designed by Isaac de Caus for the Countess of Bedford,
Lucy Harington. The roof is a shallow cross-vault, the bays
filled with strapwork in shells, with Neptunes, mermaids,
and boys on dolphins, and with a fountain on the main
wall.[34] The combination of banqueting house built over a
grotto or waterworks occurs frequently, for example at
Danvers House, Chelsea, and Whitehall (the latter by
Inigo Jones and Isaac de Caus).[35]

A rare use of a banqueting house was as a prison. The
Turret House at Sheffield Manor (Figure 18b) is reputed to
have been occasionally the prison of Mary, Queen of

Scots, during the fourteen years she was in the Earl of Shrewsbury's custody. On the few occasions she was allowed to Chatsworth on a medical visit, it is likely she was kept in a garden house there, where it would be easier to guard her.[36]

Banqueting houses could be used simply as delightful resting places during walks, places to sit, read and converse, or as places of assignation; and it was the

18(a)
Banqueting house, Temple Newsam, Leeds, 1635–6, after the engraving by Kip. The steps led to the bowling green.

18(b)
The Turret House 1570–85, the Manor Lodge, Sheffield. The banqueting room is on the top floor.

removed nature of the garden house which gave it its
dubious reputation, quite apart from the occasion of the
banquet itself when the supposed aphrodisiac nature of
many of the sweetmeats, distilled waters, and wines might
lead to amorous adventures. The puritanical Phillip
Stubbes said, in 1583, that walled gardens with their many
secret arbours and bowers and secluded banqueting
houses were just ready-made for evil-doing, especially in
towns and cities. He writes that some gentlewomen get up
late, go into town with their baskets on their arms as if to
market, but this is a subterfuge:

> In the Feeldes and Suburbes of the Cities thei have
> Gardens, either pailed, or walled around about very
> high, with their Harbers and Bowers fit for the
> purpose. And least thei might be espied in these open
> places, thei have their Banquetting Houses with
> Galleries, Turrettes, and what not els therein
> sumptuously erected; wherein thei maie (and
> doubtlesse doe) Many of them plaie the filthie
> persons ... truly I think some of these places are little
> better then the Stewes and Brothell Houses were in
> tymes past.[37]

Some city banqueting houses were well-known places of
ill-repute. In *Skialetheia* (1598), a collection of epigrams
and satires, there is reference to an old citizen 'who
comming from the Curtaine (Shoreditch) sneaketh in/ To
some odde garden noted house of sinne'.[38]

This shady reputation is further illustrated from the
seventeenth-century drama. In Shakespeare's *Measure for
Measure* (1604), the Duke's deputy Angelo lusts after the
innocent Isabella and blackmails her into promising to
spend a night with him in the garden house. In order to
save her virtue, Mariana, Angelo's erstwhile betrothed, is
substituted for Isabella in the dark. And in Massinger's *The
Bond-man* (1623), the licentious Corsica says:

> I have a couch and a banqueting-house in my
> orchard

Where many a man of honour has not scorn'd
To spend an afternoon.[39]

In *The Bloody Banquet* (1639), the lecherous Queen lures, then enjoys, the young Tymethes after an intimate banquet in 'the furthest lodge' which is clearly a banqueting house.[40]

Banqueting houses continued to be built in the eighteenth century, as much for their importance in garden design as for their banqueting function. Indeed, many are at such great distances from the house that they were more likely to be used for light day-time meals or picnics. The finest examples tend to be classical, such as the Temple of the Winds at Mount Stewart, County Down; and the temples on the terraces at Rievaulx, Yorkshire.

The serving and enjoyment of banquets From the early fourteenth century, spice dishes or plates of tin, pewter, silver, or gold, used in the void, and weighing from 6ozs to $1\frac{1}{2}$lbs, are to be found in inventories and household accounts from all parts of England—for instance the Earl of Derby's accounts in 1391 show purchases of 'spyce-plates peutre'.[41] The spice plates at court could be huge, and many. Holinshed describes an entertainment which Henry VIII gave to the French Ambassadors in 1519: after a great feast 'the king and his guests were served with . . . a *voidée* of spices, with sixtie spice plates of silver and gilt, as great as men with ease might beare'.[42]

In the later sixteenth century, spice plates appear in inventories as 'spyce treys'. The usual number in a household was four. Their shape is not specified but, in one inventory, silver spice trays have three small feet.[43] However, it is apparent from paintings that the dishes from which spices and sweetmeats were served in the early sixteenth century were usually flat and circular, and by the later sixteenth century many are saucer shaped, raised on stems. They could be made of wood or metal (pewter, silver, gold), but in the sixteenth century glass plates and dishes were usual for serving sweetmeats: either English glass, which was coarse and green because of its manufacture with burnt fern; or costly Venetian glass, which was clear and fine because of its manufacture with burnt marine plants. William Harrison is critical of his contemporaries' rage for novelty in their spurning (as too common) of gold and silver drinking vessels in favour of the new and rare Venetian glass from Murano, which could be beautifully diamond-etched and elaborated.[44] However, from 1575 glass of Venetian type was manufactured in England, when Jacopo Verzelini established a glasshouse in London. But expensive purchase was not necessary, as in the sixteenth century glass dishes could be hired for banquets.[45]

In the early seventeenth century small silver banqueting dishes for each person were usually saucer-shaped, about 6 inches in diameter, or oval, with soldered handles at each side, so that one could lift the dish to one's lips to eat wet suckets while walking about. They could be plain or given low-relief decoration in punch-work; after about 1620 they might have a scalloped rim. From about 1650 the soldered handles gave way to flat ears, and from the end of the seventeenth century banqueting plates were shaped like small waiters (salvers or trays). These were usually in silver, rarely in pewter and tin.[46] There was a special fork for eating sticky sweetmeats, with a spoon at the other end for eating syrups, jellies, and creams (Figure 13.) The sweetmeat fork was in use in England among royalty and nobles for two-and-a-half centuries before the dinner fork came into widespread fashionable use at the Restoration.

From the early sixteenth century to the mid-seventeenth century dry sweetmeats (as well as cheese, fruit, caraways, and biscuits) were eaten off small, very thin, wooden trenchers made of sycamore or beech, which look to us like tiny dinner mats only 5 or $5\frac{1}{2}$ inches in

diameter (or sometimes oblong), $\frac{1}{16}$–$\frac{1}{8}$ inch thick, painted
in black and white or bright colours with gilding, and
varnished, with elaborate decoration in cartouches and
borders. The designs were influenced by all kinds of
pattern books, emblem books, and embroideries; typical
were fruit and flowers of the months and seasons, and
signs of the zodiac. Scenes could be copied from books of
engravings, or, in the seventeenth century, engraved
scenes or coloured prints were cut out of paper and stuck
on, then varnished over.[47] By the 1580s these trenchers
included a verse or 'poesie' in the middle, and were called
roundels. Guests ate from the plain side, and at the end of
the meal everyone had to turn over their roundel and
recite the motto or sing the verse on the other side—hence
'roundelay'. These songs, riddles and aphorisms went out
of fashion during the Civil War and Protectorate. Subjects
included satirical verses, proverbs, moralising stories such
as Aesop's *Fables,* and biblical quotations. Here is an
example of late Elizabethan date from a set of roundels in
the Victoria and Albert Museum:

> Be nethyr dumbe, nor give y^i
> > tonge the lease,
> Butt speake thou well, or
> > heare and hold y^i peace.

Too often for modern taste wives and the married state are
made the subject for amusement. These are sixteenth-
century examples:

> Iff thou bee younge, then marie not yette
> Iff thou bee old thou heyste more gette
> For younge mens wives will not bee taught
> And old mens wives bee good for naught.

> Beshrewe his heart that married mee
> My wife and I can never agree
> A knavish queane by this I sweare
> The go[o]d mans breechs shee thinke to weare.

And an early seventeenth-century fable runs:

The Ape would have halfe Leonard's tayle
To hide his bum nakte as his nayle
The meaning is, such as have store
Shoulde be more liberall to the poore.[48]

Quotations from the Bible include:

All they wil lyve Godlie in Christ Jhesu must suffer
persecution 2 Times 3.

We must enter the Kingedome of God through much
troble & aflyctions [Acts 14].

Biblical quotations and exhortations to give to the poor
seem to accord badly with the sumptuousness and jollity
of a banquet. These puritanical 'poesies' were likely to
have been chosen by pious households, and used for
cheese and fruit only (though piety and sumptuousness
were not necessarily mutually exclusive).

Often given as wedding or New Year presents, trenchers
and roundels were produced in sets of six, eight, twelve,
fourteen or twenty-four in prettily decorated boxes.[49]
(Figure 13) Fine trenchers could also be made of sugar-
plate, which, when dry, could be painted in similar designs
in edible colourings bound with rosewater and gum, and
gilt.[50] Marchpanes decorated in this way could also be
used as trenchers. By breaking off a suitable emblem from
a marchpane, symbolic messages, amorous or otherwise,
could be sent to another guest, as can be seen in Thomas
Middleton's *Women Beware Women* (*c.*1625). In the
banquet scene in Act III the Ward complains of neglect
from the woman he desires:

See how she simpers it, as if Marmalad
Would not melt in her mouth: she might have had
the kindness y'faith
To send me a guilded Bull from her own Trencher,
A Ram, a Goat, or somewhat to be nibling.[51]

These astrological signs, all emblems of lust, could also
have been made out of moulded and gilded gingerbread,

marchpane, or sugar-plate. Wine glasses and goblets, as well as plates, made of sugar-plate were used on the banquet table, and were waterproof for a few hours, so long as they were not subjected to heat. 'At the end of the Banket they may eat all, and break the Platters, Dishes, Glasses, Cuppes, and all other things, for this paste is very delicate and saverous.'[52]

Gervase Markham, in *The English Hus-wife* (1615) gives instructions to the ladies of country houses as to the setting out of their banquet:

> [the] setting forth of a banquet, wherein you shall observe that March-panes have the first place, the middle place, and last place; your preserved fruits shall be disht up first, your pasts next, your wet suckets after them, then, your dried suckets, then your Marmalades, and Cotiniates, then your Comfets of all kinds, Next your Pears, Apples, Wardens, bakt raw, or rosted, and your Oranges and Lemons sliced; and lastly your Wafer-cakes. Thus you shall order them in the closet; but when they goe to the Table you shall first send forth a dish made for shew only, as Beast, Bird, Fish, Fowl, according to invention: then your March-pane, then preserved Fruit, then a past, then a wet sucket, then a dry sucket, Marmalade, comfets, apples, peares, wardens, Oranges, and Lemons sliced, and then wafers and another dish of preserved fruits, and so consequently all the rest before, no two dishes of one kind, going or standing together, and this will not only appear delicate to the eye, but invite the appetite with the much variety thereof.[53]

Even the 'housewife' according to Markham, must observe the correct ceremony; she must properly honour the food, the guests, and the occasion.

The banquet was essentially an occasion for conspicuous consumption. The adjective 'costly' occurs again and again. In palaces and great houses observers boggle at the splendour, the music, and the ceremony. Here the cupboard of gold and silver dishes, with its rosewater ewer and basin, was an essential part of the show. At Henry VIII's great feast for the French Ambassadors in 1519, which ended with a *voidée* on sixty huge silver and gilt spice plates, Holinshed says: 'This night the cupboard in the hall was of twelve stages, all of

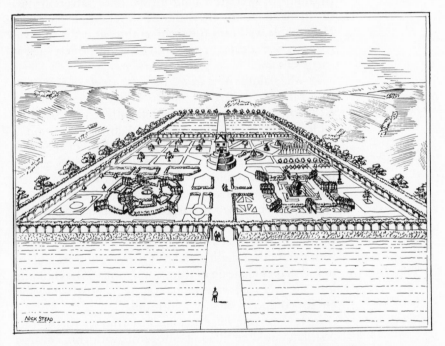

plate of gold, and no gilt plate.'[54] An account by John Strype of the lavish entertainment given to Queen Elizabeth in 1559 by Lord Arundel at Nonsuch in Surrey ends with: 'After that, a costly banquet, accompanied by drums and flutes. This entertainment lasted till three in the morning. And the Earl presented her majesty a cupboard of plate.[55]

19.
A seventeenth-century banqueting house on a mound. The drawing is loosely based on Bacon's essay 'Of Gardens' (1625). [Drawn by Nick Stead.]

However luxurious, the English banquet never

achieved the stupendous magnitude of the French banquet in the seventeenth century, when a rage for tall table decorations began about 1650 and assumed massive and towering proportions. The flowers, candelabra, and huge pyramidal arrangements of sweetstuff seemed to be an attempt to fill the vast heights of French palaces. In France this fashion ended about 1725.[56] The fashion for tall pyramids of sweetstuff built on stemmed salvers arrived in England soon after the Restoration, and stayed fashionable well into the eighteenth century. It survives today in *haute cuisine* in pyramids of confectionery such as *croquembouche*.

In Massialot's *New Instructions for Confectioners* (1692, first printed in English in 1702) there is a plan and elevation of the typical late-seventeenth-century banquet table which shows this pyramidal arrangement on a modest scale (Figure 12). The 'ground plan' of the table illustrates how closely table settings mimicked garden layouts. This example is designed for an oval table. In the middle is a hexagonal wooden or basket-work board on feet, on which are willow baskets and china dishes holding raw and preserved fruits in season. In front and behind are two oval dishes, each holding two smaller china dishes with pyramids. At either end of the oval table are club or trefoil shapes made up of three contiguous dishes holding little cups of iced waters. The four remaining flat dishes are for compotes of fruit and roots.

Instead of one large pyramid of fruit in the middle board, it could be filled up altogether with china dishes:

> that in the Middle being rais'd higher than the others, upon which several small Pyramids are to be erected of an exact Proportion: so that the same sorts of Comfits, and the same Colours may appear on every side, at the opposite Angles. Lastly, a Row or Border of raw Fruits may be made round about the Dishes, upon every Board, to garnish the top, and the whole Desert is to be set out

with Flowers, Greens, and other Ornaments, according to the Season.[57]

At banquets for fraternities and societies, Massialot suggests that the sweetmeats, biscuits, marchpanes, orange and lemon chips, dried fruits, etc. be apportioned to as many little osier baskets, decorated with 'taffety covers and ribbands', as there are guests, and that these be set out on osier boards. The most delicious comfits are put at the top. These baskets contribute to the decoration of the table during the banquet, then:

> every individual Person shuts up and takes away his Basket, to treat his Family and Friends at home; contenting himself only to eat the liquid Sweet-meats; such as Compotes and Marmelades, or else the raw Fruits, which were provided, to serve for the Out-works.[58]

It also seems to have been the custom to take home dry sweetmeats in one's handkerchief (like birthday cake in a paper napkin).[59]

Pyramids of fruit, such as cherries, were tricky to erect and so very often were formed inside conical tin moulds and the whole inverted, or built up with great care on a succession of plates. Mme. de Sévigné reports the spectacular collapse at one party of a massive pyramid, arranged on twenty porcelains, which crashed as it was being carried through the door.[60] Despite the difficulties, *service en pyramide* was *de rigueur*. In 1681 the *London Gazette* reported a glittering occasion at which there were 'four tables covered with high Piramids of all sorts of Banquet'. The pyramidal arrangements are described in 1727 by Lady Grisell Baillie in her *Household Book* after dining with Lord Mountjoy in March of that year. In a long row down the centre of the table were twelve three-tier pyramids, built of glass salvers, each having a half-inch rim. Dry sweetmeats, including apricots and French plums, occupied the lowest salvers; wet sweetmeats and jellies with covers, alternating with tall glasses, occupied the second layer; and, on the top, glasses of white comfits surrounded a 'tall scalloped glass, cornered brimmed, containing a large preserved fruit'.[61] It was usual to find from two to four of these salvers, which were low-rimmed plates on strong stems, standing one on top of another in diminishing sizes. A tall-stemmed glass containing comfits or fruit formed the apex. After mid-century, the setting out of the dessert, though still lavish, assumed a lighter and less massive appearance.

Other forms of banquet and the dessert
The term banquet could also be applied to small collations between meals. In 1509 Bishop John Fisher writes of 'Eschewinge bankettes, reresoupers, joncryes betwyxte meles'.[62] 'Rere-suppers' were rich suppers taken very late at night after the evening meal, the term being used until the early seventeenth century. 'Junkeries' in the sixteenth century referred to small feasts, or dainty dishes, or sweetmeats. In 1552 Richard Huloet refers to a 'banquet before supper',[63] and in 1620 Venner mentions 'banquets betweene meales, when the stomache is empty,' referring to a fruit banquet.[64]

This between-meals banquet was sometimes called a 'running banquet', and often consisted of fresh fruit only, whereupon it was called a 'fruit banquet'. Fruit was less expensive than sweetmeats, and so, from the late sixteenth century, a fruit banquet was popular among the middling classes, and continued so throughout the eighteenth century. In the North it survived until the 1820s. A Scottish variant was the cake and wine banquet.[65]

The term dessert first appears in the fourteenth-century *Le Ménagier de Paris* (quoted by C. Anne Wilson) where the author gives one example of a separate course of confections and fruit called *dessert* to be served before the hippocras and wafers. The word dessert comes from *desservir* — to clear the table — and it remained a French phenomenon until it appeared in England soon after the Restoration. William Vaughan in 1600 regards it as unEnglish, when he writes 'Such eating, which the French call dessert, is unnaturall'.[66] By 1666 it has been naturalised: Pepys writes in his Diary for 12 July 1666: 'The Dessert coming, with roses upon it, the Duchesse bid him try'. In the reign of William and Mary the dessert was immediately after dinner, in the form of a combined fresh fruit and sweetmeat banquet with creams and ice-creams served lavishly and ostentatiously in the drawing-room, where the guests could sit or walk about eating.

The terms banquet and dessert were both used through the eighteenth century. Sweetmeats remained in fashion (their convenient preserved nature making them easy to serve) and they were augmented with more and more fresh fruits and creams. Mrs Raffald writes in 1769:

> I have endeavoured to set out a Dessert of sweetmeats which the industrious Housekeeper may lay up in Summer, at a small Expense, and when added to what little Fruit is then in Season, will make a pretty Appearance after the Cloth is drawn and be entertaining to the Company.[67]

The 'dressing-out of a dessert' became a required accomplishment of Georgian country ladies (just as 'ordering the banquet' had been to their predecessors). In London this was left to professionals. Not all ladies were good at it — Dr Johnson wrote in 1750: 'She should be ashamed to set before company...sweetmeats of so dark a colour as she had often seen at Mistress Sprightly's'.[68]

In 1758 Horace Walpole attended a banquet at which the Prince of Wales was present when 'even on the chairs were pyramids with troughs of strawberries and cherries'.[69] Six years later, on 24 February 1764, Walpole writes a description in a letter to the Earl of Hertford of a supper he had recently attended: 'The Fairies had so improved upon it [the supper room] had so be-garlanded, so sweetmeated, and so *desserted* it, that it looked like a vision'. In this period, too, the ceremony of withdrawing for the banquet/dessert existed side by side with the simpler practice of eating it at the dinner-table, and then withdrawing for nuts and wine only, although even as late as 1800 Robert Southey wrote that the drawing-room was still 'the common place for banqueting or of eating the dessert'.[70] In the nineteenth century the term banquet dropped out of use. Dessert was eaten at the dinner-table, and the company withdrew to the drawing-room for nuts and wine only. However, even today, dons at some university colleges still leave the dinner-table on the hall dais to take their dessert, nuts, and wine in the Senior Common Room; they are a last reminder of the special institution of the banquet as it was practised and understood for three centuries.

Behaviour Banquets were often attended with games, dancing, singing and music. A Chronicle of 1548 records: 'When they had daunced, then came in a costly banket and a voidy of spices, and so departed to their lodgyng'[71]. Banquets could take place after a visit to the theatre, or theatricals take place at the banquet: by the time of Henry VIII the celebrations at Court which included a banquet might also include a masque. For example, at the Court in 1546: 'That night there was a greate banket . . . and after that, twoo riche maskes . . . and after that, a voyde'.[72] Sir Anthony Weldon, writing in 1650 about earlier events at the Court of James I, says: 'He . . . made him the most sumptuous Feast . . . that ever was seen before . . . and after that a costly voydee, and after that a Masque'.[73] Note that in 1650 the banquet was still being referred to as a *voidée*.

The picture in the National Portrait Gallery of Sir Henry Unton (1557–96) (Figure 20) supposedly at his wedding feast, shows a masque going on at a banquet, with the figures of Luna and Mercury; music is provided by a 'broken consort', which was a unique English combination of pandora, treble viol, base viol, flute, sittern, and lute, On the table are flat spice dishes and trenchers, and on the cupboard is the usual glittering display of plate, with silver rosewater ewer and basin.[47]

Phillip Stubbes, in his *Anatomie of Abuses,* was representative of the Elizabethan puritanical streak. When James I succeeded Elizabeth there was a reaction against puritanism. One example of the resulting intemperance occurred at Hatfield in June 1606 during the Court entertainments in honour of King Christian of Denmark. After the sports and great feast, there was a masque of the meeting of Solomon and Sheba (to flatter King Christian as a Solomon), which became a drunken fiasco, wonderfully described by Sir John Harington. The lady playing the part of Sheba fell over the steps to the dais and upset her casket of jewels into the Danish King's lap, 'and fell at his feet, or rather, into his face' which made a great mess and the King had to be cleaned up with napkins.

His Majesty then got up and would dance with the Queen of Sheba, but he fell down and humbled himself before her, and was carried to an inner chamber and laid in a bed of state, which was not a little defiled with the presents which had been bestowed on his garments; such as wine, cream, jelly, cakes, spices and other good matters. The entertainment and show went forward, and most of the presenters went backwards, or fell down, wine so occupied their upper chambers. Then appeared, in rich dresses, Hope, Faith and Charity. Hope tried to speak, but wine so enfeebled her endeavours, that she withdrew, and hoped the King would excuse her brevity. Faith followed her from the royal presence in a staggering condition. Charity came to the King's feet, and seeming desirous to cover the sins of her sisters, made a sort of obeisance; she brought gifts, but said she would not return home again, as there was no gift which heaven had not already given his majesty; she then returned to Hope and Faith, who were both sick in the lower hall.[75]

The proceedings ended with Victory slumped unconscious on the antechamber steps, while Peace cudgelled courtiers' heads with her olive branch.

The innocent high jinks of the Tudors, which had included such japes as 'Almeine leaps into the custard', were soon superseded by Jacobean licentiouness.[76] However, in the reign of Charles I, puritanism again took hold, and the Civil War and Protectorate made a sober interval before the Restoration saw a return to levity, when dancing replaced the masque at banquets. Both Pepys and Evelyn witnessed sumptuous sweetmeat banquets at Whitehall between the 1660s and 1680s which followed the French fashion where the spectators were kept behind a barrier while the ambassadors and honoured guests picked at the massive array of sweetmeats (which, Evelyn says, took several days in the piling up); then, at a given signal, the spectators surged forward to help themselves and the banquet was abandoned to pillage (most of it being flung about the room), the noble guests finding this sticky end all part of the entertainment.

On 22 April 1667 Evelyn witnessed the sumptuous supper in the banqueting house at Whitehall on St George's Day, with displays on the cupboard of rich plate, and music of wind instruments, trumpets, and kettle drums:

> At the banquet came in the *Queen* and stood by the Kings left hand, but did not sit: Then was the banqueting stuff flung about the roome profusely; In truth the crowd was so greate, that ... I now staied no longer than this sport began for feare of disorder.

On 18 December 1685 Evelyn dined at Whitehall Palace (the banqueting house was full of goods in storage):

> I dind at the greate entertainment his Majestie gave the Venetian Ambassadors ... The dinner was one of the most magnificent & plentifull that I have ever seene, at 4 severall Tables with Music, Trumpets, Kettle-drums &c which sounded upon a whistle at

every health: The banquet was 12 vast Chargers pild up so high, as those who sat one against another could hardly see one another, of these Sweetmeates which doub[t]lesse were some days piling up in that exquisite manner, the Ambassadors touched not, but leaving them to the Spectators who came in curiosity to see the dinner, &c were exceedingly pleas'd to see in what a moment of time, all that curious work was demolish'd and the Comfitures &c voided and table clear'd: Thus his Majestie entertain'd them 3 dayes, which (for the table onely) cost him 600 pounds.

In the sixteenth and seventeenth centuries, in a society so attuned to hidden meanings (in emblems, allusions, and conceits), the aphrodisiac nature of much of the 'banquetting stuffe' cannot have been overlooked by those providing and those partaking. It may not have been the conscious intention of the banquet-givers to serve aphrodisiacs (for instance, the Archbishop of Canterbury at Lambeth Palace, who had a banqueting house in the garden)[77] — the sweetmeats, suckets, fresh and preserved fruits and roots, sweet wines, and distilled waters would have been served out of long custom and for their deliciousness — nevertheless, the various aphrodisiac qualities attached to them (and still in use for these generative purposes in medicine) would have been known to all, adding piquancy to the proceedings, and opportunities for wit and merriment.

The aphrodisiac nature of 'banquetting stuffe'

Modern science has proved that so-called aphrodisiacs (agents used to promote sexual desire and potency) have no effect, except in the mind of the user, and that the only really effective encouragers of desire are three: imagination, intoxicants, and holidays — the latter two fostering the first. In considering banqueting, the holiday effect would be provided by the removed and idyllic atmosphere of the roof or garden banqueting house. The intoxicants, in the form of plentiful imported wines and spirits, would be augmented by the distilled waters made in the stillroom by the lady of the house from flowers, fruits, herbs and spices. Some of these waters had supposed aphrodisiac qualities. Rosa Solis, a water distilled from Sun Dew (hot and dry in the fourth degree) was popular as an aphrodisiac in Elizabethan times (though in large quantities it was discovered to be harmful and fell out of favour). Other names for Sun Dew are Lustwort or Youthwort: 'It stirreth up a desire of lust', wrote Gerard in *The Herball* 1596:

> lay the leaves of Rosa Solis in the spirit of wine, adding thereto cinnamon, cloves, maces, ginger, nutmegs, sugar and a few grains of muske, suffering it to stand in a glass close stopt from the air, and set it in the sun by the space of ten days more; then strain the same and keep it for your use.

Most of the flavourings in this recipe were considered aphrodisiacs. Clary water was another such water. Gerard said that Clary 'powdered and drunk with wine, stirreth up bodily lust'. Clary water included wine, honey, pepper, ginger, and ambergris.

Several of the spices and aromatics used in 'banquetting stuffe' and waters were considered to enjoy aphrodisiac qualities: ginger, used in hippocras and gingerbreads, 'provoketh sluggish husbands';[78] zedoary, of the ginger family, pepper, cumin, caraway, coriander, aniseed, pine kernels,[79] cloves 'stir up Venus';[80] saffron 'provokes Venus';[81] ambergris from the sperm whale and musk from the gland of the male musk deer had both been used as perfumes and flavourings and in aphrodisiac preparations since ancient times. The hot, dry qualities of these spices and aromatics, added to the hot, dry quality of dried fruit and sugar, were thought to heat the blood and inflame the Original Fire. Thomas Tryon declared in 1696 that young people:

> ought to avoid the eating of all sweet compounded Foods, and drinking of strong Cordial Drinks, for

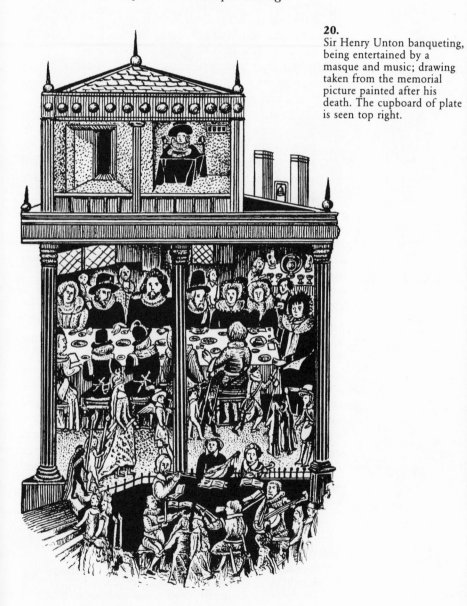

20.
Sir Henry Unton banqueting, being entertained by a masque and music; drawing taken from the memorial picture painted after his death. The cupboard of plate is seen top right.

such things heats their Blood, irritates their Spirits, sets open the Gates of *Venus,* putting Nature and all the Propertie into an unequal operation.[82]

Potatoes were also well-known aphrodisiacs. William Harrison gives a good description of banquets among gentlefolk and merchants about 1577–87, adding:

> Of the potato and such venerous roots as are brought up out of Spaine, Portingale, and the Indies to furnish up our bankets, I speak not, wherein our Mures [Murrens?] of no less force, and to be had about Crosbie Ravenswath, doe now begin to have place.[83]

The sweet potato, brought to Spain in the early sixteenth century, was imported by London shops and sold as a delicacy. The Virginia potato (our ordinary potato) and Canada potato (Jerusalem artichoke) arrived in the later sixteenth century and early seventeenth century respectively, and were candied by confectioners as a delicacy in much the same way.[84] The remark in 1601 by Clusius to the Papal Legate about Spanish potatoes could apply to all three: 'they are flatulent, and therefore some use them for exciting Venus'.[85]

Eringo roots (Sea Holly), 'the bignesse of a man's finger, and very long' (Gerard), were similarly candied with rosewater, orangeflower water, or cinnamon water and musk, both by apothecaries and confectioners. Gerard wrote that they were good for those 'that have no delight or appetite to venery'. Kissing comfits were made out of Eringo roots. Falstaff mentions these three supposed aphrodisiacs in *The Merry Wives of Windsor,* V.v, when he goes to Windsor Forest to meet Mistress Ford:

Mtrs Ford: Sir John! art thou there, my dear, my male deer?

Falst: My doe with the black scut! Let the sky rain potatoes; let it thunder to the tune of 'Green Sleeves', hail kissing-comfits and snow eringoes; let there

come a tempest of provocation, I will
shelter me here. (Hugs her).

Other venerous roots which could appear at the banquet
in sweet composts were parsnips, and carrots, 'a great
furtherer of Venus her pleasure':[86]

Marmalade of quinces, once considered medicinal as
an aid to digestion after a meal, became by 1608 (*A Closet
for Ladies and Gentlemen*) a pretty 'banquetting conceit',
but its luxuriousness gave it a special venereal
connotation. Two recipes in that book fortify other,
literary, references: for example, 'soft marmalade hearts'[87]
and 'marmalade lips'.[88] Queen Mary Tudor's Marmalade
(to help her conceive a son) included sugar, quinces,
candied orange peel, almonds, candied eringo roots,
musk, ambergris, rosewater, cinnamon, ginger, cloves and
mace. (Almonds were thought to foster fertility.)[89] The
second recipe was also intended to promote the
generative powers. It included ginger, eringo roots, cocks'
stones (testicles), rocket (*Brasica eruca*, an aphrodisiac
much used in the Middle Ages), red nettle seeds (long
used as an irritant), *scincus marinus* (a lizard regarded by
the Ancients as aphrodisiac), and diasatyrion (an
electuary made of dogstones, that is orchis root, which was
also an aphrodisiac). Other restoratives included were
gold leaf (aphrodisiac) and powdered pearl.[90] Finally,
'marmalade madams' in the late seventeenth and
eighteenth centuries became an epithet for prostitutes.[91]

Artichokes were aphrodisiac, preserved in sugar syrup;[92]
chestnuts were 'windy' and so stimulated lust;[93] apples,
pears, pomegranates, figs, and prunes were venereal.[94]
Andrew Boorde wrote in 1542: 'Fygges ... stere a man to
veneryous actes, for they doeth auge and increase the
seede of generation'.[95] Prunes set in the window was a sign
of a brothel; stewed prunes were a particular dish in
brothels.[96] And an immoderate use of chocolate in the
seventeenth century was thought to be aphrodisiac:[97]
chocolate was prepared with vanilla, another aphrodisiac.

According to the Rev. Richard Warner, sexual stimulus could be present at the banquet in visual form. Writing in 1791, he is critical of the grossness of former times, and condemns that sixteenth-century 'indecent appendage', the codpiece of 'enormous magnitude', as worn by the well-dressed gentleman. He goes on:

> The *table* also exhibited strong proofs of this grossness of manners, which ... pervaded the greater part of Europe. Hence arose an extraordinary species of ornament, in use both among the English and French, for a considerable time; representations of the *membra virilia, pudendaque muliebria,* which were formed of *pastry,* or *sugar,* and placed before the guests at entertainments, doubtless for the purpose of causing jokes and conversation among them: as we at present use the little devices of paste, containing mottos within them, to the same end. *Vide* Le Grand's [Legrand d'Aussy's] *Histoire de la Vie Privée de François* Tom II 269.[98]

The intimate relationship between food and sex which must have been implicit in all Tudor and Stuart banquets, because of the aphrodisiac nature of much of the 'banquetting stuffe', is here made plainly and unequivocally manifest.

Notes

1. Richard Warner (ed.) *Antiquitates Culinariae* (London 1791), pp.xli and 93, note, reprinted by Prospect Books: 'Within an owre the King askid the voidee, and drank, the travers yn the chambure edraw, and every man depairtid and went to rist.' (*A ... Cronycle of the Dethe and False Murdure of James Stewarde, Kynge of Scotys,* translated by John Shirley, 1440 [1818].) The void could also be taken mid-afternoon, after a mid-day dinner.

2. *A Collection of Ordinances and Regulations for the Government of the Royal Household ...* (London, Society of Antiquaries, 1790), p.36;
   > Then the Yeoman of the Ewrie must take up the Table cloth, the Usher must see the Tables, chayres and stooles taken away in order. Then the Lorde must drynke Wyne standyng, and all other in lyke manner,

and that done, every man departeth at his good
pleasure. [*The Inthronization of Archbishop Nevill* (1466),
quoted in Warner, pp.104–5.]

3. If the lord or lady had only one or two guests they would take
    the void sitting, in a small private chamber, see *Sir Gawain
    and the Green Knight,* modernised by J. R. Tolkein, (London,
    1975), p.26, quoted in Mark Girouard, *Life in the English
    Country House* (New Haven and London, 1978), p.32.

4. The complicated and time-consuming ceremonial of serving
    the void at the Court of Henry VII is described in *The Articles
    Ordained for the Regulation of the Household of Henry VII (A
    Collection of Ordinances . . .,* p.113, and Warner, p.xli); see also
    Warner, p.93, note, and Froissart's *Chronicles,* tom.II cap. 164,
    fol. 184a, cap. 100 fol. 114a.

5. Girouard (1978), pp.30, 49, 94, 104. Cardinal Wolsey calls to
    Sir Thomas Lovell, 'is the banquet ready I'th privy chamber'
    after the clearing of the main meal from the presence
    chamber at Wolsey's St James's Palace in York Place.
    (Shakespeare, *Henry VIII* I, iv. 98.)

6. G. B. Hughes, 'The Old English Banquet', *Country Life,* CXVII,
    17 February 1955, p.474 (gives no references).
    In developing the banqueting house for the new banquet
    course, the Tudors must have had as a precedent the idea of
    the medieval gloriet, which was a highly decorated room or
    suite of rooms in a castle, often in a tower. The gloriet could
    also be a pavilion or lodge set in a pleasance or pleasure
    garden, which might be on an island in a lake, or moated, or
    it could be a hunting stand set in a glade to view hunting, or
    a fishing lodge to view fishing. Waterworks, fountains,
    fishtanks, and aviaries were a feature of some of these. As late
    as 1450 a castellated pavilion was planned for Richard
    Beauchamp's new park at Bronsil near Ledbury in
    Herefordshire. So it seems that from the Middle Ages onwards
    there was a continuous use of lodges, pavilions, and summer
    houses, which from about 1530 became specialised into rooms
    where one ate the sweet banquet, without necessarily losing
    their original function. (See J. H. Harvey's entries on
    pleasance and gloriet in *The Oxford Companion to Gardens,*
    1986.)

7. Roy Strong, *The Renaissance Garden in England* (London, 1979)
    p. 28 and illustration on pp.26-7.

8. James Lees-Milne, *The Tudor Renaissance* (London, 1951), p.49;
    Miles Hadfield, *A History of British Gardening* (London,
    1960), p.43; and Emily Lu Pearson, *The Elizabethans at Home*
    (Stanford, 1957), p.62; their description conflicts with that of
    Strong (1979, p.39 and note), who says that at Nonsuch there
    was an elaborate two-storey banqueting house on a mount
    with balconies on the first floor, its roof decorated with the
    king's beasts, see the description in *Surrey Archaeological*

Collections 5 (1871), p.146, and John Dent, *The Quest for Nonsuch* (London, 1962), p.113ff. Strong says ... (p.68) there was also at Nonsuch a wooden banqueting house, a Bower of Diana in the Grove of Diana, probably built by Lord Lumley in the 1570s. Thomas Platter reported it as vaulted and containing a marble table. It was totally rebuilt 1622 (PRO E 351/3244: 1609–10; and PRO E 351/3255).

9. Lees-Milne, pp.51–3.
10. Mark Girouard, *Robert Smythson and the Elizabethan Country House* (New Haven and London, 1983), p.46; The Records of the building of Longleat, II, p.121.
11. Hadfield, p.43.
12. Girouard (1978), p.25.
13. Girouard (1978), p.106.
14. *Robert Laneham: A Letter of 1575*, ed. F. Furnivall (London, 1907), p. 50.
15. Lees-Milne, p.112.
16. 'The Smythson Collection of the R.I.B.A.', ed. M. Girouard, *Architectural History*, 5, (1962), pp.51, 134. Also illustrated in Girouard (1983).
17. 'Smythson Collection', *Architectural History*, 5, (1962), p.37.
18. Hadfield, p.69, *Parliamentary Survey*, 1649 in J. Caley, *Archaeologia*, 10, (1792), pp.419-20.
19. John Parkinson, *Paradisus Terrestris* (London, 1629), p.610, quoted in Strong, pp.69–70.
20. Lucy Aikin, *Memoirs of the Court of Queen Elizabeth*, (London, 1819), p.274.
21. Francis Bacon, *Essays Civil and Moral*, Essay No. XLVI, 'Of Gardens' (1625).
22. *Aubrey's Brief Lives*, ed. Oliver Lawson Dick (Peregrine, 1962), pp.123–4.
23. John Worlidge (J. W. Gent), *Systema Agriculturae* (London, 1681).
24. John Rae, *Flora, Ceres and Pomona* (London, 1662).
25. F. G. Emmison, *Tudor Secretary: Sir William Petre at Court and at Home* (London, 1961), p.35.
26. John Smyth *Lives of the Berkeleys* (1618) ed. Sir. J. MacLean (Gloucester, 1883), II p.362, quoted in Girouard (1978), p.106.
27. John Buxton, *Elizabethan Taste* (London, 1963), p.20.
28. N. Pevsner, *Buildings of England: North Somerset and Bristol* (London, 1958), p.274.
29. N. Pevsner, *Buildings of England: Essex* (1954), fig.53.
30. Girouard (1978), p.106, from Richard Carew of Anthony, *The Survey of Cornwall, etc.*, ed. F. E. Halliday, (London, 1953), pp.175–6.
31. Paul Hentzner, *Travels in England during the Reign of Queen Elizabeth* (London, 1889), pp.52–3.
32. Hughes, pp.474–5.

33. Journal of Thomas Dineley, *Kilkenny Archaelogical Society* n.s.4 (1862–63), pp.105–6. Christopher Wren and Hugh May were asked advice by Ormonde about making this fountain, see Edward Malins and the Knight of Glin, *Lost Demesnes — Irish Landscape Gardening 1660–1845*, (London, 1976), p.6.

34. Barbara Jones, *Follies and Grottoes*, 2nd edn (London, 1974), p.145. Strong, p.140.

35. Strong, pp.178–9.

36. Mary Walton, *The Prisons of Mary, Queen of Scots, in Yorkshire and Derbyshire*, Sheffield City Libraries Local Studies Leaflet.

37. Phillip Stubbes, *Anatomie of Abuses* (1583), ed. F. J. Furnivall (New Shakespeare Society, London 1877–9), p.87.

38. E. Guilpin *Skialetheia* (London, 1598).

39. Phillip Massinger, *The Bond-man* (1623), ed. Gifford (1840) I.iii. p.93, col.1.

40. *The Bloody Banquet* (1639) (Malone Society Reprints, 1961).

41. Hughes, pp.474–5.

42. Holinshed, *Chronicles*, p.849 a. 40. See Warner, p.xli.

43. Hughes, pp.474–5.

44. William Harrison, *[Description of England] Elizabethan England*, ed. Lothrop Withington, intoduction by F. J. Furnivall, p.147, The Scott Library 50.

45. Hughes, pp.474–5. Duke of Rutland's MSS 1598.

46. Hughes, pp.474–5.

47. Owen Evan-Thomas, *Domestic Utensils of Wood* (London, 1932), p.67 has illustration of trenchers reproducing Jan van de Velde's 1621 copies of Marcus Gheeraerts the Elder's illustrations for Lucas d'Heere's book of fables, *De Warachtign Fablen der Dieren* (Bruges, 1567).

48. Evan-Thomas, pp.64–66; G. Puttenham, *The Art of English Poesie* (1589) says:
    There be also another like epigrams that were sent usually for New Year's gifts or to be printed or painted on banketting dishes of sugar plate or of March paines etc. they were called 'Apophoreta' and never contained above one verse or two at the most, but the shorter the better. We call them poesies and do paint them nowadays upon the back sides of our fruit trenchers of wood.

49. Jane Toller, *Treen* (London, 1975), p.26; Edward H. Pinto, *Treen* (1968), pp.79–80 and figs. 61, 76, 77, 188; G. Bernard Hughes, 'The Use of Trenchers', *Country Life*, 27 August 1953, p.630.

50. Sir Hugh Platt, *Delightes for Ladies* (1605), A38; T. Dawson, *The Second Part of the Good Hus-wives Jewell*, (1597), p.40.

51. Thomas Middleton, *Women Beware Women*, (1625) ed. Charles Barber (Edinburgh, 1969), III.i.80.

52. Dawson (1597), p.40.

53. Gervase Markham, *The English Hus-wife*, 4th edn. (1631), p.98.

54. Warner, p.xli.

55. Quoted in Warner, p.xlvi.

56. Barbara K. Wheaton, *Savouring the Past: The French Kitchen and Table* 1300–1789 (London, 1983) p.188.

57. François Massialot, *New Instructions for Confectioners* (London, 1702), p.126; John Nott, in his *Cook's Dictionary* (1723), plagiarises Massialot's chapter on the setting out of a banquet or dessert.

58. Massialot, p.125.

59. Middleton, III.ii.303.

60. Wheaton, p.188.

61. Lady Grisell Baillie, *The Household Book 1692–1733,* ed. R. Scott-Moncrieff (Edinburgh, 1911), p.298.

62. Bishop John Fisher, Funeral Sermon of the Countess of Richmond 1509 *Works,* I (Early English Text Society, ES 27, 1876) p.294. 'Junket' remained a general name for any sweet confection, and 'junketing' for banqueting or merrymaking.

63. Richard Huloet, *Antecoenium* (Abecedarium Anglicum Latinum, 1552).

64. Tobias Venner, *Via Recta ad Vitam Longam* (1620), V p.91.

65. Hughes, pp.474–5 and illustrations.

66. William Vaughan, *Naturall and Artificial Directions for Health,* 7th edn. (1633), II.ix.54.

67. Elizabeth Raffald, *The Experienced English House-Keeper,* (Manchester, 1769), p.362.

68. Samuel Johnson, *The Rambler* No 51, p.6.

69. Quoted in Hughes, pp.474–5.

70. Ibid.

71. Edward Hall, *Chronicle* (1548), p.99.

72. *State Papers during the Reign of Henry VIII ,* xi, 1546, (London 1852), p.262.

73. Sir Anthony Weldon, *The Court and Character of King James* (1650), p.19.

74. Girouard (1978), p.89, plate VII; Roy Strong, 'Sir Henry Unton and his portrait', *Archaelogia* 99, (1965), plate 26; Roy Strong, *The Cult of Elizabeth* (London, 1977), p.104.

75. Quoted in Philippa Pullar, *Consuming Passions* (Sphere, 1972), pp.128–9.

76. Warner, p.130; *All's Well that Ends Well,* II.v.40; Ben Jonson *The Devil is an Ass,* I,i,95ff. The Almain was a kind of dance. The Almain or Almeine leap into a custard was a speciality of Lord Mayor's banquets.

77. A deliberately aphrodisiac banquet is prepared by the Queen for Tymethes in *The Bloody Banquet,* (1639), III,iii,1093. Roxano as pandar, addresses Tymethes:
    > This banquet from her owne hand received grace
    > Her selfe prepar'd it for you; as appeares
    > By the choyce sweetes it yeelds, able to move
    > A man past sence, to the delights of love.

78. Henry Buttes, *Dyets Dry Dinner* (London, 1599); Jane O'Hara May, *Elizabethan Dyetary of Health* (Lawrence, Kansas, 1977), p.273.

79. Pullar, pp.237–9.
80. Thomas Cogan, *Haven of Health* (London 1612), p.123.
81. O'Hara May, p.273.
82. Thomas Tryon, *Wisdom's Dictates* (London, 1696), p.9.
83. Harrison, p.148. Mures, or Murren, was Bryony, *Bryonia dioica,* the native English equivalent of true Mandrake. Mandrake, the famous magical root of the Ancients, was popularly believed to help women conceive (though Gerard ridiculed the idea).
84. Parkinson, p.518; R. N. Salaman, *The History and Social Influence of the Potato* (Cambridge, 1949), p.104.
85. Salaman, p.104.
86. Pullar, pp.237–9.
87. Thomas Middleton, *Blurt Master-Constable* (1602), III.i.
88. Philip Massinger, *The Picture* (1629), I.i.
89. A. Wilson, *The Book of Marmalade, (London* 1985) pp.42–4.
90. H. S. Denninger, 'A History of Substances known as Aphrodisiacs', *Annals of Medical History,* 2, (1930), p.388; Wilson, pp.42–4; John Davenport, *Aphrodisiacs and Anti-Aphrodisiacs,* (London, 1869), pp.102; 110; Pullar, pp.237–9.
91. Wilson, pp.42–4.
92. Wheaton, p.67.
93. Buttes (1599); Pullar, p.237.
94. M. P. Cosman, 'A Feast for Aesculepius: Historical Diets for Asthma and Sexual Pleasure', *Annual Review of Nutrition* 3, (1983), p.1–33.
95. A Boorde, *A Compendyous Regyment, or A Dyetary of Helth, 1542,* ed. F. J. Furnivall, (Early English Text Society, ES 20, 1870) c.21.
96. *2 Henry IV,* II.iv.143; *Measure for Measure,* II.i; 88–9; Thomas Dekker, *Seven Deadly Sins of London* (London, 1905) p.49; *Captain Underwit,* IV.ii. in *A Collection of Old English Plays,* ed. A. H. Bullen (London, 1882–5), II, 377.
97. Davenport, p.90.
98. Warner, p.136.

Index

158

Index